BREATH OF ANTI-CHRIST

THE BREATH OF ANTI-CHRIST

Exposing the Strategy Behind the Destruction Aimed at Every Human Being on Earth–Including You

VERN PELTZ

The Breath of Anti-Christ

Copyright © 2016 by Vern Peltz. All rights reserved.

No part of this publication may be reproduced, stored in a retrieval system or transmitted in any way by any means, electronic, mechanical, photocopy, recording or otherwise without the prior permission of the author except as provided by USA copyright law.

Scripture quotations marked (amp) are taken from the *Amplified Bible*, Copyright © 1954, 1958, 1962, 1964, 1965, 1987 by The Lockman Foundation. Used by permission.

Scripture quotations marked (kjv) are taken from the *Holy Bible, King James Version*, Cambridge, 1769. Used by permission. All rights reserved.

Scripture quotations marked (niv) are taken from the Holy Bible, New International Version®, NIV®. Copyright © 1973, 1978, 1984 by Biblica, Inc.™ Used by permission of Zondervan. All rights reserved worldwide. www.zondervan.com

Quotations taken from Dake's Annotated Reference Bible: Quoted by Permission. Dake's Annotated Reference Bible. The Old and New Testaments with Notes, Concordance and Index © Copyright 1963 by Finis Jennings Dake. Dake Bible Sales, Inc., Lawrenceville, Georgia.

Original word definitions used by permission: A Concise Dictionary of the words in The Greek Testament; with their renderings in the Authorized English Version by James Strong, S.T.D, LL.D. L A R I D I A N Cedar Rapids, Iowa Copyright. King James Version Exhaustive Concordance of the Bible Electronic Files Copyright © 2004; by L A R I D I A N. All Rights Reserved.

Dictionary definitions:

The New Strong's Exhaustive Concordance of the Bible. Copyright 2001 by Thomas Nelson Publishers. Used by permission of Thomas Nelson Publishers. All rights reserved.

Quotations taken from Barna: Quoted by Permission. The Barna Group. 2368 Eastman Ave. Unit 12, Ventura, California 93003. United States.

Quotation taken from *End of the American Dream*: Quoted by Permission. *End of the American Dream* endoftheamericandream.com.

This book is designed to provide accurate and authoritative information with regard to the subject matter covered. This information is given with the understanding that neither the author nor Tate Publishing, LLC is engaged in rendering legal, professional advice. Since the details of your situation are fact dependent, you should additionally seek the services of a competent professional.

Cover design by Norlan Balazo
Interior design by Shieldon Alcasid

Published in the United States of America ISBN: 978-1-68301-236-8
1. Religion / Christian Life / Spiritual Warfare
2. Religion / Christian Theology / Angelology & Demonology
16.07.25

Contents

Introduction 7
1   The Spirit of Antichrist 11
2   Characteristics of Society 43
3   Characteristics of the Last-Day Church 53
4   Have You Been Affected? 93
5   Lawlessness 105
6   Wisdom 125
7   This is How We Know! 139
8   Paul's Concern 153
9   My Concern 165
10 What's the Answer? 171
11 What is Our Hope? 179

Introduction

As a pastor, I am asked about my opinion concerning the End Times—or the last days—on a regular basis. There are many opinions of how things will unfold during this time. In reality, we won't know for certain until we get there. This is an not another book looking at the issues of how close we are to the return of Jesus, when the tribulation will begin, whether it will be worldwide, etc. This book is looking at this time from a whole different perspective.

I have been bothered for sometime with the attitudes of society as well as the complacency, lethargy, and self-absorption of the church. One of the key things Jesus warned about concerning the time we live in is deception. We are told over and over in the scriptures to watch out for it and guard against it. Yet it seems that the average person, whether they are a believer or an unbeliever in Jesus, feels somehow we have an immunity to what Jesus was warning us about. The feeling seems to be: we are not deceived, nor will we be deceived. At the same time, I'm watching not only our society, but also the Christian church grow less and less passionate about God, God's opinions, His desires, what pleases Him, and how much He or His Word should even influence us in how we live as a society or a believer.

I personally have no desire to be deceived. But equally with that and possibly even greater, I am deeply concerned about our children, grandchildren, great-grandchildren, and on into our lineages until Jesus returns. I believe what Jesus and the apostles warned us about is accurate. Deception is growing thicker with every year that goes by.

The problem with deception is this: the people who are deceived rarely recognize it. That's why it's called deception.

In an effort to find some principles that would protect myself, my family, my church, and anyone else who is willing to listen, I believe the Holy Spirit has given some insight that has not only changed my life, but I believe will change the life of every person who sees what He has shown to me.

The Apostle Paul said there is a "secret power of lawlessness" that is at work in America and the world (2 Thessalonians 2:7). What is it doing? What does it look like? How can we recognize it? Is there anything we can do to protect ourselves from it? Can it be stopped?

I believe what is laid out in the following pages will impact you the same way it impacted me the first time I saw it. There is an enemy that is seducing everyone on planet earth. To defeat this enemy, we must become aware of it and understand it. The Lord Jesus wants to give new insight into this enemy. Once you see it, you'll never be the same.

We are in the End Times, and what the scripture has warned us to watch for is happening around us on a daily basis. This book is a fresh perspective that scripturally identifies the *real danger* that is facing this world, society, and especially the church of Jesus Christ.

Thank-You for reading this book. I pray this insight changes you and everyone upon whom you have an influence.

> The problem with deception is this: the people who are deceived rarely recognize it. That's why it's called deception.

1

The Spirit of Antichrist

Antichrist. That is the word or name that we have heard a lot about over the last few decades. Who or what are we really talking about? Most of us would probably think about a man named Antichrist—the number *666*, the world coming to an end—things like that. Even though we know, according to scripture, there is a man coming who will be called "the Antichrist," I'm not going to be talking about him in this book. I'm going to be looking at the spiritual atmosphere or spirit of the age that is going to usher the man called the Antichrist into power. Whether the man who will be called the Antichrist is rising toward power at this time, we don't know; but we do know the "spiritual force or power" that will propel him into power is active among us right now. John told that to us in 1 John 4:3.

This power or spiritual atmosphere is spoken of a number of times in scripture. We're going to look at a few places that address it very directly. Let's begin by looking at the book of 1 John. Interestingly, John is the only one to use the word *Antichrist* anyplace in the New Testament (kjv). So this book is a good place to start.

Before we take a look at the specific sections of scripture that deal with Antichrist, let me describe what I mean by "Breath of Antichrist." The phrase is taken directly from 1 John 4:3(niv). Here's what it says: "But every spirit that does not acknowledge Jesus is not from God. This is *the spirit of the antichrist*, which you have heard is coming and even now is already in the world."

Did you see it? It's italicized in the verse above: "the spirit of the Antichrist." Many people don't understand what that means, so let's do a word study on it based on *Strong's Greek Dictionary of the New Testament*.

Spirit

> 4151. πνευμα pneuma, pnyoo'-mah; From 4154;
>
> *A current of air,* that is, *breath* (blast) or a breeze; by analogy or figuratively *a spirit,* that is, *(human)* the rational soul, (by implication) vital principle, mental disposition, etc., or
>
> (superhuman) *an angel, demon, or (divine) God, Christ's spirit, the Holy Spirit."*

This Greek word *pneuma* is very literally defined as a breath. It seems to be the word that most closely defines what the beings of the spirit realm are like, whether they are human spirits, angelic spirits, or demonic spirits. This is the word that is used to describe what they are. In a bit, I'll explain how that pertains to us and our lives. Let's look at the next words.

Antichrist

> 500. ἀντίχριστος antixristós, an-tee'-khris-tos;
>
> From 473 and 5547; *an opponent of, an imposter for the Messiah.* :—*antichrist.*"

Christ

> 5547. Χριστός Xristós, khris-tos';
>
> From 5548; anointed, that is, the Messiah, an epithet of Jesus. :—Christ.
>
> 5548. χρίω xriō, khree'-o;
>
> Probably akin to 5530 through the idea of contact; to smear or rub with oil, that is, (by implication) to consecrate to an office or religious service. :—anoint.

This is what we are seeing in this verse:

1. Please take note of this: John says the spirit to which he is referring was already in the world when he wrote the book of 1 John. So this is not the man called Antichrist. This is dealing with a spirit or spiritual atmosphere. I believe it's talking about the same realm to which Paul was referring in Ephesians 2

and 6. In Ephesians 2:2 (niv), Paul calls it "the ruler of the kingdom of the air." When he talks about it in chapter 6, he said we are wrestling against "the spirit forces of wickedness in the heavenly (supernatural) sphere" (Eph. 6:12, *Amplified*).

2. The word *spirit* shows us that the supernatural realm is around us everywhere, just like the air of the physical realm. However, the spirit realm that John is talking about here is not God and His angels. John is talking about the devil and his kingdom. We know that because of the word *Antichrist*. The Antichrist isn't God's idea. This thing is of Satan.

3. The word *Antichrist* is referring to something that is opposed to or against Christ.

4. We know the word Christ means, "the anointed one, and His anointing. The Messiah." It comes from the Greek word number 5548. It is the word used for anoint or anointed, which, you can see from the definition above, means to "smear or rub with oil."

In 1 John 4:3, he called this evil the "spirit of the Antichrist." Directly translated from its original language it would read this way: the "breath (spirit) of the Anti-anointing/Messiah (Christ)."

This is a summary of what is being described in the phrase "spirit of Antichrist." We are surrounded by a spiritual atmosphere that is opposing Christ (the Messiah, the anointed one and His anointing). It is devilish in origin. It is thick around us, like the physical air or atmosphere we breathe. However, this is not physical; this is spiritual. It is rubbing and smearing on us like an oil. It's an unholy, counterfeit anointing. Its focus, goal, and purpose is to hinder and thwart the true anointing, which comes from Jesus the Messiah.

So what is it trying to accomplish? We know its general purpose is to be against God and what He's trying to do on this earth. But what really is its focus? Here is what every person on earth is facing. Satan's attack is ultimately on the gift of eternal life that God has offered to mankind. He will do everything he can to make sure we either never get it or we lose it.

Add to that problem, the time or age in which we are living. We are in the End Times. It's in our era that wickedness/lawlessness takes a giant spike in intensity. Here are a couple of verses that point that out:

> Because of the increase of wickedness, the love of most will grow cold, but he who stands firm to the end will be saved. (Mt 24:12–13, niv)

> For the secret power of lawlessness is already at work; but the one who now holds it back will continue to do so till he is taken out of the way. And then the lawless one will be revealed. (2 Thes 2:7–8, niv)

These two—(1) the spirit of Antichrist and (2) the increase of wickedness and lawless—will work together like a team to accomplish one ultimate goal. What is the ultimate goal that Satan is after?

The book of 1 John really brings clarity to the ultimate goal of this evil of our time. It will ultimately be the same goal of the "man" who will be known as the Antichrist. To find the answer to that question—what is the ultimate goal?—let's begin by looking at how John describes what is going to be happening in the time leading up to the revelation of the man Antichrist.

What is John trying to tell us? I will enlarge on it as we work through the subject, but in a nutshell he is saying two things:

1. the statement in itself is saying the ultimate purpose of this time will be to undermine, discredit, and disprove the Messiah. It's an all-out concerted effort to convince mankind that Jesus *is not* the Christ,

2. he is saying that this anti-Messiah or anti-anointing influence will be in the spirit realm. It surrounds us like breath or air. This thing is of Satan. It literally permeates the atmosphere that surrounds us. It emanates from the evil side of the spirit realm and will be continually trying to move people toward the belief that *Jesus* is not *the Christ*. Or at the very minimum, that *Jesus* is not *the* only *Christ*.

To say it another way, John is telling us that the Antichrist spirit will be promoting the concepts:

1. Jesus is not *the way* of salvation for the human race, and/or
2. Jesus is not *the only way* of salvation for the human race (there are other ways to God).

Let's take a deeper look at what John had to say about it in 1 John 2:18–27 and 4:1–6.

> 18 Dear children, this is the last hour; and as you have heard that the antichrist is coming, even now many antichrists have come. This is how we know it is the last hour. 19 They went out from us, but they did not really belong to us. For if they had belonged to us, they would have remained with us; but their going showed that none of them belonged to us. 20 But you have an anointing from the Holy One, and all of you know the truth. 21 I do not write to you because you do not know the truth, but because you do know it and because no lie comes from the truth. 22 Who is the liar? It is whoever denies that Jesus is the Christ. Such a person is the antichrist—denying the Father and the Son. 23 No one who denies the Son has the Father; whoever acknowledges the Son has the Father also. 24 As for you, see that what you have heard from the beginning remains in you. If it does, you also will remain in the Son and in the

> Father. 25 And this is what he promised us—eternal life. 26 I am writing these things to you about those who are trying to lead you astray. 27 As for you, the anointing you received from him remains in you, and you do not need anyone to teach you. But as his anointing teaches you about all things and as that anointing is real, not counterfeit—just as it has taught you, remain in him. 28 And now, dear children, continue in Him, so that when He appears we may be confident and unashamed before him at His coming. 29 If you know that He is righteous, you know that everyone who does what is right has been born of Him. (1 John 2:18–29, niv)

There are a number of things we should notice here.

Verse 18. Even back in John's time, the process was underway. He was also part of the last times, and this was proven by the many people who are *anti* the *Christ*. They had fallen under the pervasive power of this time. In this

> It's an all-out concerted effort to convince mankind that Jesus is not the Christ.

section of scripture, John is talking about people who have become Antichrist, or literally *anti the Christ* (the Messiah, the anointed one and his anointing). In chapter 4, he's going to switch emphasis a little and address the spiritual atmosphere that is at work behind the scenes, which is producing this anti-Jesus or anti-the-Messiah people. He's going to call that supernatural atmosphere the *Antichrist spirit*.

Verse 19. A division was and still is taking place because of the people who have been influenced by the Antichrist spirit. John describes them as either belonging to the church or not belonging. If they have left, it was an indication that they didn't really belong to or weren't a part of the church.

Belong here is an important word. It comes from two Greek words (*Strong's* G1510 and G2258) that indicate "I exist in agreement." It is telling us that like in John's time, these people are not existing in agreement. (They didn't belong.) There is going to be disagreement that is associated with this spiritual force of Antichrist and the people who come under its power. (At this point, we're not sure what he means by that, but he will tell us.) However, we do know this much: this disagreement begins in the church!

Verse 20. This has to do with an anointing and the truth. He states here that the people who have remained true to the church and Jesus have the anointing of the Holy One (Jesus). They know the truth. So, evidently, some so-called Christians will carry an anointing that is not from Jesus, and as a result they won't know the truth. They'll be deceived, and likely that's why they leave the church. That's what we are warned about over and over concerning the last days—deception (Matt. 24:4–5, 11, 24; Mark 13:6, 22; Luke 21:8; 2 Thess. 2:3; 1 Tim. 4:1; 2 John 7; Rev. 13:4).

Verse 21. The reason John is writing these people is because they know the truth. Therefore, he can explain this to them. They know the truth, so they will recognize what he's about to say as truth. The truth cannot lie, so he can't be deceiving them.

Verse 22. The real liar and deceiver is the person who denies Jesus is the Christ (the Messiah, the anointed one.). Messiah means the "only Way" or the "only one" who provides salvation. If we deny Jesus as being the "the Way" or the "only Way" of salvation, John says we are an Antichrist (we are a person who is *anti* the true or holy anointing). This is something that we are seeing become more and more prevalent in our lifetime (especially in America). It is the concept that says Jesus is not the *only way* of salvation. And sad to say, it's being pushed more and more not only in our society, but also in the church. The Holy Spirit knew this would happen, so He prophesied it through John.

> The real liar and deceiver is the person who denies Jesus is the Christ.

Verse 23. If we deny that Jesus is the only way to God (the Messiah), then we don't have God the Father. On the other hand, if we do acknowledge that Jesus is the Son of God (the Christ, the Messiah), then we have the Father.

This is an absolutely huge principle. In light of what is happening around us now, this verse is an enormous mouthful. What John is actually saying is the opposite of a belief that is gaining popularity in the world right now. John is exposing the heart and soul of the ultimate goal of Satan and his Antichrist system. Do you see it?

John is saying that if we do not accept Jesus as the Messiah or the only way to the Father, then we are not serving the same God. So it's not possible for Christians and Muslims to be serving the same God. It's not possible for one group of people to get to the Father through Allah and the other group get to the same Father through Jesus. *John is saying if we don't come to the Father through Jesus, we don't have the same Father. That same principle is true for any religion.*

Buddhists and Christians don't serve the same God. Hindus and Christians don't serve the same God. (you fill in the religion) and Christians don't serve the same God. The Holy Spirit is warning us that in the last days, people will be saying that everyone serves the same God. We simply get to him through different avenues. Some get to God through Buddha, some get to him through Allah, some feel the access is Ishvara, but in the end we're all serving the same God.

This is the ultimate deception of the Antichrist spirit and person will try to instill. This is the core of the spirit of Antichrist.

And John says anyone who holds this belief system is an Antichrist. They are the liars (v. 22).

Verses 24–25. John says we need to guard the message that was given earlier about Jesus being the Son of God and the only way to the Father. This is what will keep us connected to the Father. This keeps us in our salvation and will give to us what He promised: eternal life.

Verse 26. There is a group of people who are saying it doesn't work this way; there are other ways of salvation besides Jesus. I presume this is the same group of people who eventually left the church because of the disagreement that arose concerning whether or not a person can get to the Father without Jesus (v. 19).

Verse 27. However, as for the true church of Jesus (true believers), we have received the true anointing from Him, and it is in us. We don't need anyone to teach us who our salvation comes through. This anointing we've received teaches us that it comes through Jesus. This anointing we received from Jesus is

> The Holy Spirit is warning us that in the last days, people will be saying that everyone serves the same God. We simply get to him through different avenues.

real. It will teach us about *all* things. We need to follow what it has taught us about the source of salvation (Jesus) and remain in that understanding because there is a *counterfeit* anointing that is teaching something different. That counterfeit anointing is the spirit of Antichrist (anti-anointing).

Please notice something here: John is calling the spirit of Antichrist an *anointing*. It is a counterfeit anointing, which makes it an unholy anointing. But nonetheless, it is an anointing. This goes back to what I said before: the spiritual atmosphere that is around us is rubbing and smearing on us like an anointing. Its purpose is to deceive us. And the ultimate deception would be to convince us that there is more than one way to God.

It's that counterfeit anointing (Antichrist anointing) that is teaching people the wrong things and leading them astray. It is a lie. It is the reason people are leaving the church and going off to believe there are other ways of being saved. (This will become more prevalent during the time in which we are living.)

Because this is happening, we can't simply believe everything that comes along. We must learn to test the spirits. That way, we can identify the Antichrist spirit. Before John goes into talking about testing the spirits (ch. 4), he tells us how to test the spirits (ch. 3).

Verse 28. As believers, we are to continue in Christ so that we will be ready for His coming.

Verse 29. If we know Jesus is righteous, then we can also know that people who do what is right are born again. The transition John is making here is very important. It will tie into the principles he gives in chapter 3 for testing for the Antichrist spirit. Remember: this is one letter that John wrote. He was talking about the Antichrist in chapter 2. He talks about it some more in chapter 4. Chapter 3 is not a different subject. John hasn't changed the subject. He's talking about Antichrist all the way through. Chapter 3 is part of the whole discussion.

When you take the whole book of 1 John in context, like it should be, chapter 3 becomes a very heavy chapter. John lays the groundwork that is used to test the spirits. Please keep something in mind here: in context, John is not talking about casting out demons, deliverance sessions, or anything like that. He's showing us how to recognize the difference between an Antichrist spirit and the true Spirit of God. In chapter 3, John gives some major principles that are used to test for the Antichrist spirit. Let's look at chapter 3, and then we'll point out these principles.

> 1 How great is the love the Father has lavished on us, that we should be called children of God! And that is what we are! The reason the world does not know us is that it did not know Him. 2 Dear friends, now we are children of God, and what we will be has not yet been made known. But we know that when He appears, we shall be like Him, for we shall

see Him as he is. 3 Everyone who has this hope in Him purifies himself, just as he is pure. 4 Everyone who sins breaks the law; in fact, sin is lawlessness. 5 But you know that He appeared so that He might take away our sins. And in Him is no sin. 6 No one who lives in Him keeps on sinning. No one who continues to sin has either seen Him or known Him. 7 Dear children, do not let anyone lead you astray. He who does what is right is righteous, just as He is righteous. 8 He who does what is sinful is of the devil, because the devil has been sinning from the beginning. The reason the Son of God appeared was to destroy the devil's work. 9 No one who is born of God will continue to sin, because God's seed remains in him; he cannot go on sinning, because he has been born of God. 10 This is how we know who the children of God are and who the children of the devil are: Anyone who does not do what is right is not a child of God; nor is anyone who does not love his brother. 11 This is the message you heard from the beginning: We should love one another. 12 Do not be like Cain, who belonged to the evil one and murdered his brother. And why did he murder him? Because his own actions were evil and his brother's were righteous. 13 Do not be surprised, my brothers, if the world hates you. 14 We know that we have passed from death to life, because we love our brothers. Anyone who does not love remains in death. 15 Anyone who hates his brother is a murderer, and you know that no murderer has eternal life in him. 16 This is how we know what love is: Jesus Christ laid down his life for us. And we ought to lay down our lives for our brothers. 17 If anyone has material possessions and sees his brother in need but has no pity on him, how can the love of God be in him? 18 Dear children, let us not love with words or tongue but with actions and in truth. 19 This then is how we know that we belong to the truth, and how we set our hearts at rest in his presence 20 whenever our hearts condemn us. For God is greater than our hearts, and He knows everything. 21 Dear friends, if our hearts do not condemn us, we have confidence before God 22 and receive from Him anything we ask, because we obey His commands and do what pleases Him. 23 And this is his command: to believe in the name of his Son, Jesus Christ, and to love one another as He commanded us. 24 Those who obey his commands live in Him, and He in them. And this is how we know that He lives in us: We know it by the Spirit He gave us. (1 Jn 3:1–24, niv)

Verse 1. John immediately begins to talk about the love of the Father and how His great love for us has made us his children. He explains the reason for the division between the world and believers. The reason: they don't know the Father or the love of the Father.

Verse 2. We are His children, and when He appears, we shall be like him and truly see Him for who He is.

Verse 3. Everyone who is making this their goal purifies themselves. The standard of purity we use is the standard of purity He has set. He is pure.

Verse 4. Breaking the law is sin. In fact, sin can be summed up as lawlessness. *This point is very important. It will show up numerous times as we put this whole picture together.* I will be referring back to this verse later in the book.

Verse 5. Jesus came to take away our sin. He personally has no sin.

Verse 6. If we know God and live in him, we cannot continue to live in sin. The truth is the person who continues in their sin has not seen God nor do they know Him. The transition that John is making into talking about sin—which began in chapter 2 verse 29—is not an accident. Please don't miss this. Continuing to live a life of sin is one of the principles John looks for to recognize the spirit of Antichrist. Watch as John develops on this principle.

Verse 7. John says here is a principle that will keep you from being deceived. A righteous person does what is right, just as Jesus is righteous.

> Breaking the law is sin. In fact, sin can be summed up as lawlessness.

Verse 8. The person who does what is sinful is of the devil because the devil has sinned since the beginning. That's why Jesus came—to destroy the devil's work. In verses 8–9,

John has now drawn the line between righteousness and unrighteousness. This is a very important distinction of which we must take note. *Deception creeps in when we begin calling right as wrong and calling wrong as right. This is a foundational principle for recognizing deception in the last days.*

> *The tone of society will be to say that what scripture declares to be "right" is actually "wrong," and what scripture declares "wrong" is actually "right."*

Verse 9. Anyone who is born of God cannot continue to go on living in their sin. Please be sure to tie this together in your mind. Remember, sin is lawlessness (v. 4), the devil is lawless (tie v. 4 to v. 8), and God considers people who sin to be lawless (v. 4). This is a principle that is to be used in testing the spirits to see if it is of God or if it is an Antichrist spirit. (Again, this will become more clear as we go on, but please make a mental note of it.) Now just in case there are any misunderstandings, John gets really blunt in verse 10.

Verse 10. Remember: in context he is still talking about the Antichrist spirit. The children of God would have the true anointing (1 John 2:20). The children of the devil would have the counterfeit anointing, or the Antichrist spirit (1 John 2:27b). Now John shows us how we can tell

---

Deception creeps in when we begin calling right as wrong and calling wrong as right.

who is from which anointing: who the children of God are and who the children of the devil are. It all goes back to doing what's right or doing what is sin. If we do not do what is right, we are not a child of God. And we are also not of God if we don't love other Christians. This person would be of the devil and under the Antichrist spirit. Notice: according to this verse, the hatred of Christians and Jews has its roots in the Antichrist spirit ("anyone who does not love his brother"). Anyone who is under its influence is literally taking on the attitude and mind-set of the Antichrist anointing.

Wow! That's being direct.

Now John is going to begin to talk about love for God and love for one another. How does that tie into the Antichrist spirit? We know that Jesus told us that the first commandment was to love God, and the second was to love other people (Matt. 22:37–40). Since the Antichrist spirit is against God, it will be against what Jesus commanded. So love will be a huge principle in recognizing the Antichrist spirit and who is under its influence.

Verse 11. Everything revolves around *love*, especially in human relationships.

Verse 12. Cain killed Abel. This happened because of a lack of love. Cain's actions were evil.

Verse 13. The world hates. It's the way of the world. Don't be surprised if the world hates the believer.

Verse 14. The test to know under which spirit we are operating is this: do we have love for other Christians? A foundational test to know if someone is saved or not is if we love other believers. Anyone who hates other believers is in death.

Verse 15. That hate makes them murderers. They have no eternal life in them. With that in mind, under which kingdom are they operating (God's or the devil's)? By which spirit (or anointing) are they being influenced (God's spirit or the Antichrist spirit)? To make a direct application, Muslims cannot say they hate Christians and Jews but still claim we have the same God—via Abraham. This is a deception. If the same spirit was operating in the Islamic faith that was operating in the Christian/Jewish faith, Muslims would be moved to love the Christian and the Jew. But since the anti-Semitic/anti-Christian sentiment is ever increasing—to the level of physically murdering Christians and Jews—according to the principle John just laid out, the Islamic faith has no eternal life in it.

Verse 16. True love is laying down our life for other believers. It does not use God as a justification to kill others who don't think like it does. True love follows the example

> Muslims cannot say they hate Christians and Jews but still claim we have the same God— via Abraham.

of Jesus and lays its life down for others, especially for fellow believers.

Verse 17. True love influences how we take care of each other in the physical realm.

Verse 18. Love is more than words. It comes out in actions. Many times our actions speak more truthfully than our words.

Verse 19–20. This is how we know we belong to the truth—we love in action and deeds. If we really understand this, it will set our hearts at rest, even in those times when we're questioning and feeling condemned. This is tying back into chapter 2 verse 19. To whom do we belong? Do we belong to the truth and the church or not? How could John know that the people who were leaving the church in chapter 2 verse 19 did not belong to it? He is telling us in chapter 3 verses 16–20. The people of chapter 2 didn't belong to the truth because they didn't love with actions and truth. That's why he could say, "They left us but they never belonged to us." They weren't living in true love. And to whom did he say in chapter 2 verses 20–23 that they belonged? Antichrist. That's the spirit they were a part of. So one way to test the spirits and know if it is of God or of Antichrist is to see if

> Here is His command: believe that Jesus is God's Son, and He is the source (the Christ, Messiah) of our salvation, and to love each other.

the people are walking in love. (The kind described in chapter 3 verses 11–24.) Any motive or action that is of God (the true anointing) does not hate and murder each other. The true Spirit of God will cause people to lay their possessions and lives down for each other, not hate and kill each other. The refusal to help each other—the hating and killing of others—is not of God. It is of the Antichrist spirit.

Verse 21–22. Answers to prayer come from confidence before God, asking Him, obeying His commands, and doing what pleases Him.

Verse 23. Here is His command: believe that Jesus is God's Son, and He is the source (the Christ, Messiah) of our salvation, and to love each other.

Verse 24. If we obey, He lives in us, and we in Him. We know this by the Holy Spirit who lives in us. If we do not obey what He said in verse 23, He is not influencing and living in us. That leaves only one other spirit that these people can be under: Antichrist spirit.

Let's review. This is important. Here are some of the principles that John has just pointed out that are necessary to test the spirits. He has given us a number of principles to determine if someone is of the true spirit of God or under the influence of the Antichrist spirit. Here is a summary of those points:

1. We can only know God and who the other believers are via love (v. 1).

2. Sin and lawlessness are the same thing (v. 4).
3. As a believer, we cannot continue to live a life of sin (v. 6).
4. Whoever continues in a lifestyle of sin is of the devil. They are not of God (vv. 7–10)—sinning by not loving God enough to obey Him and do what's right; sinning by not loving others, especially other believers.
5. We know someone has eternal life if they love (not hate) others. Anyone who simply hates someone else is considered a murderer in God's mind (vv. 11–15), much less the actual act of physically murdering someone. To kill someone simply because they are not of your religion is a foundational proof you don't know the true God, nor are you saved.
6. Love takes action. It's not just talk. It lays down its possessions and even its own life for others (vv. 16–20).
7. The evidences that we belong to God are these: we obey His commands (vv. 22, 23), we do what pleases Him (v. 22), we believe Jesus is the Son of God, the Messiah who is the source of our salvation (v. 23), and we love each other (v. 23).
8. We personally know He lives in us by His Holy Spirit who lives in us (v. 24).

Now John goes back to talking about the Antichrist spirit. In chapter 3, he just gave us some principles to use in testing. Now he's going to make direct application and show us how to test for the Antichrist spirit.

> 4:1 Dear friends, do not believe every spirit, but test the spirits to see whether they are from God, because many false prophets have gone out into the world. 2 This is how you can recognize the Spirit of God: Every spirit that acknowledges that Jesus Christ has come in the flesh is from God, 3 but every spirit that does not acknowledge Jesus is not from God. This is the spirit of the antichrist, which you have heard is coming and even now is already in the world. 4 You, dear children, are from God and have overcome them, because the one who is in you is greater than the one who is in the world. 5 They are from the world and therefore speak from the viewpoint of the world, and the world listens to them. 6 We are from God, and whoever knows God listens to us; but whoever is not from God does not listen to us. This is how we recognize the Spirit of truth and the spirit of falsehood. (1 Jn 4:1–6, niv)

Before we go on, I need to make sure you are recognizing something. Do you remember the definition of the word *spirit*? The title *spirit* can be referring to God, Jesus, the Holy Spirit, the devil, angels, demons, and humans. All of us have one thing in common: we are all spirits. The Greek word "pneuma" (definition given above) is used to refer to all of them. Here are some examples:

God–John 4:24; Romans 8:9, 14; 15:19; 1 Cor. 2:11; 3:16; 2 Cor. 3:3. (All references to the Spirit of God, which is the Holy Spirit–who is God)

Jesus–Mark 2:8; 8:12; Luke 23:46; 24:39; John 13:21.

Holy Spirit–Matthew 10:20; 12:28; Mark 1:10; Luke 2:27. (All references to the Holy Spirit)

Devil–Ephesians 2:2; 6:11-12.

Angels–Hebrews 1:7, 14.

Demons–Matthew 12:43; Mark 1:23-26; 9:17-26; Mark 5:2, 8; Luke 4:33; 8:29.

Humans–Matthew 26:41; Luke 1:47, 80; 8:55; 9:39-42; John 4:23-24; 1 Thess. 5:23.

In John chapter 4 verse 2, the spirit that John is testing to see if it is of God or of the devil (Antichrist spirit) is the human spirit. He's revealing how we can tell if a person is under the influence of the Antichrist spirit or not. An example of that type of influence getting on a human can be found in Matthew 16:23. Peter was making a statement to Jesus, and Jesus immediately knew the influence Peter was under. The source of Peter's thinking and statement was Satan. Recognizing that, Jesus said: "Get behind me Satan" (niv). So it is possible for a human being to be directly influenced by an ungodly spirit. There are also many examples we could give where people have been influenced by the Holy Spirit. The point is this: In the book of 1 John, he is showing us how to recognize if a person has come under the influence of the Antichrist spirit. He has shown many characteristics of what a person thinks and acts like when they are under the spirit of Antichrist.

So in chapter 4 verse 2–3, when he's talking about testing the spirits, he is again showing us how to determine if a person (human spirit) is under the influence of God or under the influence of the Antichrist spirit (the devil). When John says "every spirit that acknowledges" (v. 3), or "every spirit that does not acknowledge" (v. 4), he's talking about a human being. He's referring to a human being either acknowledging Jesus as the Messiah or denying Jesus as the Messiah. This is not talking about a demon or some other type of spirit. The principles that we laid out above from chapter 3 are some of the things we look for to make this determination. John tells us how we can know which spirit a person is under (God's or Antichrist's). In context, this is not talking about demonic spirits that need to be cast out, etc. It is talking about the overall spirit of Antichrist and the influence it's having on people (human spirits). The glaring issue of 1 John chapters 2-4 has to do with people and what is going to happen in the world of human beings in the last days. This is not revealing how to find out if a demon is anti the Christ or not. That's a no brainer. All of the demonic realm is anti Jesus, or anti the Christ. The greatest last days deception has to do with the human being deciding whether they are for Jesus being the

Messiah / Christ, or are they anti the Messiah / Christ. We can test people in order to know what they really believe. John has already given us numerous characteristics to look for, but he's about to give us another HUGE test. With that in mind, let's go through the first verses in chapter 4.

Verse 1. Just because a prophet is saying something doesn't mean it's of God. Test what is being said. Because of the Antichrist spirit and how it affects people, there are many people who have become false prophets.

Verses 2–3. Take this verse in context of what John said in chapter 2. He was talking about the source of our salvation—the Messiah. Here he says the Spirit of God will say that Jesus came in the flesh. Remember to connect that statement with chapter 2 and why he came to this world in the flesh. He came as our Messiah and Savior. Tie this back into the Gospel of John chapter 1, where it is talking about Jesus having come in the flesh. What does it say there as to why he came? To be the Light and Life of our salvation. He came to bring salvation (Messiah).

So John is still on the same theme. Salvation cannot come through anyone other than Jesus the Christ (the Anointed One, the Messiah).

> *This is going to be a huge issue in our future. This will be the culminating issue before Jesus's return. The issue: is Jesus the Way or only Way of salvation?*

Those who are under the influence of the Antichrist spirit will say *no*, Jesus is not *the* Way or *the only* Way.

The Antichrist spirit is fighting against the anointing and the Messiah, so anyone who has been influenced by it will deny that Jesus came in the flesh and became *the only* Savior of mankind (which Jesus himself professed [John 14:6]). If this simple yet major point is not acknowledged—which I state again: Jesus is *the only Messiah or Savior* of the human being—then we can know that person is under the influence of the breath of the anti-anointing/Antichrist. In fact, in chapter 2, John said this person is an Antichrist (v. 22).

> Those who are under the influence of the Antichrist spirit will say Jesus is not "The Way" or "The Only Way" of salvation or eternal life.

Verse 3. The spirit of the Antichrist was already beginning its work in the world when John was alive. So we know he's not talking about the man who is called the Antichrist. He's talking about a spiritual influence, which is exerting continual pressure upon us and surrounds us like the physical air we breathe.

Verse 4. True believers have overcome this line of reasoning that does not acknowledge Jesus as the only Messiah or Savior. Believers have overcome it because of the anointing of Jesus (the Holy Spirit) that lives within them. (Again, refer to chapter 2 verses 21 and 26–27.)

Please notice something: John is equating *them* with the *one who is in the world*. In context, the one who is in the world would be the spirit of Antichrist, and the one in us who is greater than the one in the world is the Spirit of God. Why would he say that? Why say that these people (*them*) are the same as the Antichrist spirit, and as believers we must (John says they *have*) "overcome them"? The reason is that he's not talking about some nebulous spiritual force that is floating around somewhere-out-there as the only problem. *He's saying this spirit of Antichrist gets on and in people. It changes them.*

It changes how they think, what they believe, how they act, what they do, and how they talk. The spirit that's in them will come against the true believers through these people. In chapter 4 verse 1, he called them false prophets. In verse 2, the spirit he's talking about is the human spirit. He's talking about human beings. People speak what they truly believe (2 Corinthians 4:13). They speak it out of the deepest part of their being—their heart (Matthew 12:34–35). When human beings refuse to accept that Jesus is the only Messiah for the world, John is saying that this person is the spirit of Antichrist. (They are one with the spirit. They have been influenced to believe like it and talk like it.) These are the people to whom he's referring when he says: "You, dear children, are from God and have *overcome them*."

Verse 5. The Antichrist spirit and the people under its influence are from the world. They will speak from the viewpoint of the world, and the world will listen to them (there will be agreement).

This is the counterpart to what John spoke about in chapter 2 verse 19, where John says that the people who didn't really belong to them didn't stay with the church. They left it. They are the same ones he's talking about in the next verse (v. 6). These people left them, and they would not listen to them. The people who are under the influence of the Antichrist spirit belong to the world and will listen to it and speak like it. *They don't want what the scripture or the Holy Spirit have to say. Here John is giving another principle that we can use to test the spirits of people.*

Verse 6. When it comes to this issue of through whom salvation comes (which has been the main focus of chapter 2 verse 18 through chapter 4 verse 6), John says *the people who know God, His anointing* (chapter 2 verse 21 and verses 26–27), *and His Spirit* (chapter 3 verse 24 and chapter 4 verse 2) *will listen to the ones who are proclaiming that Jesus is the only way to heaven: that He is the only Messiah. This is how we recognize the Spirit of truth. These people are not deceived or under the counterfeit anointing* (chapter 2 verse 27). *They are not under the delusion and influence of the spirit of Antichrist. This is how we recognize the spirit of truth and the spirit of falsehood.* (In context: spirit of falsehood is referring to the spirit of Antichrist.) *Again we are being shown how to test the spirits of people to know whether they are under the Antichrist spirit or not.*

The people who don't listen to this message of Jesus being the only Way to the Father or agree with it are not of God. They are of the counterfeit anointing (chapter 2 verse 27). *They are of the spirit of falsehood. They are of the Antichrist spirit* (chapter 4 verse 3). *They are the ones to whom John was referring in chapter 2 verse 19—the ones who left them (the church). THIS IS THE MAIN WAY WE RECOGNIZE AND TEST THE SPIRIT OF ANTICHRIST.*

The people who are under the Antichrist spirit say that Jesus is not the only Messiah or the only way of salvation. This is the ultimate goal Satan has in mind, and it's the main reason for what the spirit of Antichrist is doing in the earth today. Its goal is to deceive people into not believing what Jesus said: "Jesus saith unto him, I am the way, the truth, and the life: no man cometh unto the Father, but by me" (Jn 14:6, kjv).

That is the influence that literally flows through and emanates from the *air or spirit* world around us. Its ultimate goals are to attack the anointing and the fact that Jesus is the only way of salvation (the Messiah).

Now we know the main objective *of what is happening in the evil side of the spirit world* which infiltrates the air around us and is trying to influence people to believe its way.

But how will it operate in order to desensitize and deceive everyone in the world so we believe it (including Christians [Matthew 24:22–24])? It's simple to see that you can't just have people make the jump from being solid believers in Jesus to denying he is the only way, or even a way at all. What will happen to people who slide away from the truth? What is capable of blinding them into believing this ultimate lie?

If the spirit of Antichrist is alive and well among us—and we know it is because of what John said in chapter 4 verse 3—then we should be able to determine the avenue through which it will try to influence and deceive society by simply looking at what society will be like in the last days.

> The ultimate goals of the spirit of Antichrist are to attack the anointing and the fact that Jesus is the only way of salvation (the Messiah).
>
> Now we know the main objective of what is happening in the evil side of the spirit world, which infiltrates the air around us.

2

Characteristics of Society

As the Holy Spirit was showing all of this to me, this was my question: how did we get to this point? What could be happening in society, or in the church, that would open the door to this level of deception? Believe it or not, the Bible tells us. And once you see it, I believe it will leave you shocked and in amazement.

We will begin by looking at some of the characteristics of what society will be like in the last days. Let's start with Second Timothy.

> 1 But mark this: There will be terrible times in the last days. 2 People will be lovers of themselves, lovers of money, boastful, proud, abusive, disobedient to their parents, ungrateful, unholy, 3 without love, unforgiving, slanderous, without self-control, brutal, not lovers of the good, 4 treacherous, rash, conceited, lovers of pleasure rather than lovers of God—5 having a form of godliness but denying

its power. Have nothing to do with them. (2 Tim 3:1–5, niv)

The Holy Spirit, through Paul, really does a very insightful job of laying out the attitudes of society in the last days. Here the Holy Spirit is revealing in plain English what the spirit of Antichrist will cause people and society to be like. This scripture is not just talking about unbelievers. It's talking about what *people* (v. 2a, 5b) will be like. That means there will be Christians like this also.

Let's go through this verse by verse.

Verse 1. Now the things that Paul listed here have been around for most of the history of mankind. But evidently, something will be different about these things because Paul says: "But mark this: there will be terrible times in the last days." So even though these things have been around for a long time, I would say something has taken a dramatic turn for the worse.

Before we go through the rest of the verses, let me share with you how this came to me. I was studying the subject, and as a result, I was looking at this portion of scripture. I read the first line, "People will be lovers of themselves," and the Holy Spirit made a statement to me. He said, "There is the summary of everything Paul listed here."Then he asked me a question. He asked, "Is there anything in that list that does not originate with selfishness?" The more I look at the scriptures, the more I realize the title to this list could be *selfishness*. Let's look at it.

Verse 2. *Lovers of themselves*: selfish. In fact, the *Amplified Bible* translates it as "utterly self-centered."

Lovers of money. How many people work hard to accumulate a lot of money with the sole intent of giving it away? The average person wants money so they can keep it or spend it on themselves. What are we looking at? Selfishness.

Boastful. What does the average person brag about? What are they proud of? Typically, it has something to do with them or making them look good. So the intent is selfish.

Proud. This is simply identifying the core of what we brag about. Pride has to do with self-exaltation. Generally speaking, the things the average person is proud of have to do with something or someone that makes them look good. Again, selfishness (all about me).

Abusive. Why do people abuse others or things? The reasons usually somehow revolve around wanting to dominate, control, or force someone/something to be a certain way. What is that way? More than likely, it has to do with what they want. Again, it's about getting their way (selfishness).

Disobedient to their parents. Why is the average child disobedient to their parents? Because they don't like something, they don't want to do it, or their desires are different. (Again, it's selfishness.)

Ungrateful. Ungratefulness usually comes from thinking we deserve whatever we were given. It comes from an entitlement mentality: "Why should I be grateful? This is what I expected." (Selfishness) It should be coming to me. It's all about *me* and how deserving I am.

Unholy. This word is defined as *wicked*. This will be explained under 2 Thessalonians 2. But again, it has to do with being selfish.

Verse 3. Without love. The King James Version and the *Amplified Bible* translate it as "natural affection" or "natural human affection, callous and inhumane."

The Greek definition in *Strong's* (G794) defines it as, "hard hearted towards kindred." For a practical definition: *Kindred* is typically defined as "family or some type of relationship by blood."

Why do we become cold, callous, and indifferent toward our family (hard-hearted)? As a pastor, I find it usually has to do with something that is being required of us that we don't want to give, or something with which we don't want to agree. It's all about *us* in what we want or what we think, and very little about the other person. It's called selfishness.

Unforgiving. Why don't we forgive? We may be *that* angry. We may want revenge. We want the other person to pay for what happened. Whatever the reason, we feel justified in our position. It's about our hurts, feelings, pain, regret, distrust, etc. It's all centered around us. It's selfishness.

Slanderous. Defined as "false accuser" (*Strong's*). Why would we falsely accuse someone?

Why not just say the truth? Likely, the reason is because it will somehow turn out better for us if we don't say the truth. Somehow, we're looking out for our self. Selfish.

Without self-control. Why don't we control ourselves? Because we don't want to (selfish).

Brutal. Brutal carries the connotation of being violent. We can be verbally brutal, physically brutal, etc. What causes a person to be like that? What causes someone to violate another person? I highly doubt it has anything to do with being concerned about the other person. Again, this whole thing is about me, my feelings, my anger/rage, etc. It's selfishness.

Not lovers of the good. Why is it when something about morality or righteousness is brought up in a conversation, it typically turns into a big argument? A lot of people don't want to hear it (try Facebook for example). The reason they don't want to hear it typically has to do with the fact they want to do their own thing. They don't want any standards or absolutes governing their lives. They want to do what they want, when they want. Sounds familiar? Yeah, it's selfishness.

Verse 4. Treacherous. In other translations, this is translated "betrayers." Again, we have a characteristic of selfishness. When we betray, in some way we are usually looking out for our own interests. We don't betray others with their best interests in mind.

Rash. Rash is when we are not carefully considering the consequences of an action. This can be linked to being too impulsive. It can be simply looking for the gratification of the moment without giving much thought to any aftereffects. No matter how we try to define it, again we will find that rash people are making decisions and taking action focused on how it will affect them. Somehow they believe they will benefit by the quick decision or action that is about to happen.

Conceited. To be conceited is to be proud of or enthralled with yourself. Sounds like selfishness to me.

Lovers of pleasure rather than lovers of God. This point is pretty much self-explanatory. Here a person is focused on their own pleasure, or what will make them happy, rather than the dedication and commitment needed to be loyal to God's purpose and pursuits. We are first. God comes later. Selfishness.

Verse 5. Having a form of godliness but denying its power. This easily makes sense when you put it in the context of the Antichrist spirit. The power of God comes from the anointing of the Holy Spirit. So to be against Christ (the Messiah, the Anointed One and his anointing) would automatically pit us against His power. So the Antichrist spirit actively works to cause people to deny, not allow, disavow, or simply take a stand against the power of the Holy Spirit. Why would people do that? There can be numerous reasons, but if you boil them all down to the core, I think you'll find it revolves around self. Maybe it came from a disappointment, an unanswered prayer, a second- or third-person offense, seeing little supernatural in their own lives; ministers do it to remain loyal to an organization, etc. Whatever the core reason, the result is usually rooted in "this isn't working for me, so I'm going to do it my way." Or as in the case of a minister, this supernatural stuff could get me into trouble with my denomination, my church, or even some of my best friends. It will be better for me, my family, and my career if I just stay away from it. Whatever the reason, when we distance ourselves from the power of God or supernatural, we're usually protecting ourselves in some way. Again, it's rooted in selfishness.

No matter how you look at that section of scripture, there is a clear tone of selfishness found through it. Here is another scripture that deals with selfishness and society.

> 34 Be careful, or your hearts will be weighed down with *dissipation, drunkenness* and the *anxieties of life*, and that day will close on you unexpectedly like a trap. 35 For *it will come upon all those who live on the face of the whole earth.* 36 Be always on the watch, and pray that you may be able to escape all that is about to happen, and that you may be able to stand before the Son of Man. (Lk 21:34–36, niv)

In this scripture, Jesus is warning us of something that will come up on the whole earth. Let's look at the four things he listed (all four definitions are from *Strong's Concordance*):

1. *Dissipation* (G2897, kjv—*Surfeiting*)

    "A headache or seizure of pain from drunkenness. This word signifies the giddiness and headache resulting from excessive wine-bibbing, a drunken nausea."

2. *Drunkenness* (G3178)

    "Apparently a primary word; an intoxicant, that is, (by implication) intoxication."

3. *Anxieties* (G3308, kjv—*Cares*)

    [solicitude: care]
    "To draw in different directions, distract, hence signifies that which causes this, a care, especially an anxious care."

4. *Life* (G982)

    "Relating to the Present Existence; Things that Pertain to this Life."

It is apparent that in the last days, there will be a lot of intoxication by either alcohol or drugs. The reason I add drugs to that statement is because of the definition in number 2 above. Drugs also act as an intoxicant. So I believe the definition gives leeway to include drugs into this last days scenario. The reason people are turning to the drugs and alcohol has to do with the pressures, cares, and worries of living our lives—our present existence. For whatever reason, life will become so heavy and so overwhelming that in these people's minds, the only pleasure or escape becomes some form of intoxication. Jesus is directly warning mankind about getting caught in this trap.

Application: when life gets tough, our way of handling it is to get smashed or high (turn to alcohol or drugs). This is a scary scenario. Is this response focused on our wife, family, marriage, job, career, etc. Who is it all about? This response is focused on finding relief for one person—me. No matter how negatively this may affect others in my life, the choice is basically a selfish decision, response, choice.

Selfishness is the main characteristic that is driving society in the last days.

I don't think it takes a genius to look at society and see that we are increasingly becoming a selfish society. But here is the big question that was going through me: was selfishness successful in getting into the church? Let's look at that next.

3

Characteristics of the Last-Day Church

There are numerous scriptures that warn believers concerning the last days. In these warnings, we can find characteristics of what this time period will look like. So let's look at a few of them.

> 3 As Jesus was sitting on the Mount of Olives, the disciples came to him privately. "Tell us," they said, "when will this happen, and what will be the sign of your coming and of the end of the age?" 4 Jesus answered: "Watch out that no one deceives you. 5 For many will come in my name, claiming, 'I am the Christ,' and will deceive many. 9 Then you will be handed over to be persecuted and put to death, and you will be hated by all nations because of me. 10 At that time many will turn away from the faith and will betray and hate each other, 11 and many

false prophets will appear and deceive many people. 12 Because of the increase of wickedness, the love of most will grow cold, 13 but he who stands firm to the end will be saved. 14 And this gospel of the kingdom will be preached in the whole world as a testimony to all nations, and then the end will come. 36 No one knows about that day or hour, not even the angels in heaven, nor the Son, but only the Father. 37 As it was in the days of Noah, so it will be at the coming of the Son of Man. 38 For in the days before the flood, people were eating and drinking, marrying and giving in marriage, up to the day Noah entered the ark; 39 and they knew nothing about what would happen until the flood came and took them all away. That is how it will be at the coming of the Son of Man. 42 Therefore keep watch, because you do not know on what day your Lord will come. (Mt 24:3–14, 36–42, niv)

Verses 4–5. Deception will be running rampant. The problem with deception is that it is so difficult to recognize. Deception is not blatant. It is subtle. People who are deceived don't realize they're deceived. It becomes a blinder over their eyes. They can't see it. They believe the way they are thinking and running their lives is normal for a Godly person.

Christians who are deceived are extremely difficult to help. No matter how obvious the deception is to people around them, they are blind to it. The only one who can point out the error and show them the deception is the Holy Spirit. If an individual tries to point out error to another believer—unless the Holy Spirit is involved in the situation convincing and persuading the person—what usually happens is they will rationalize and justify their choices and behaviors. It's very difficult to help them see what people around them are seeing.

> People who are deceived don't realize they're deceived. It becomes a blinder over their eyes. They can't see it. They believe the way they are thinking and running their lives is normal for a godly person.

This may be difficult to understand, but one of the main reasons we are deceived is because we wanted to be deceived. We wanted to believe something so badly that when the opportunity came, we simply gave in to the opportunity. Allowing deception to get into our lives has a lot to do with our own desires, ambitions, and greed. We're wanting something badly enough that we're willing to believe just about anything so that we can have it. That's why the roots of deception are firmly planted in selfishness.

Verse 9. Hatred of, persecution of, and death will be prevalent for people who believe in and follow Jesus. Why would this be? It's because a true follower in Jesus has standards and morals and takes a stand for righteousness.

A true disciple will be proclaiming that Jesus is the only way to salvation. As we've already discovered from the book of 1 John, this is not a popular message in the last days. The further we get into this time period, the more intense the hatred, persecution, and betrayal of true believers will become. And just like Jesus said, it will be because of Him. So in order to protect our own interests (selfishness), many people will fall into what is stated in verse 10.

Verse 10. Many people back away from Christianity and their faith in Jesus. They will betray and hate other believers (presumably a result of verse 9).

Verse 11. However, prophecy (via religious people, fortune-telling, etc.) will be prevalent. These prophets will also work in deception. It's part of what the Holy Spirit warned us about in 1 Timothy 4:1–2 and 2 Timothy 4:3–4 (again, deception is tied to selfishness).

This point is very interesting to me. As I look around, I ask myself where are all the prophets in the secular world in America? There are very few. So when Jesus says many false prophets will arise and deceive many people, it makes me ask, how many of these are going to be in the church? At this point in time, this can't be talking about the secular realm. Why do I say that? Let me ask this question: how many prophecies do you hear about that are currently coming out of the secular world? I don't know of many. Prophecies are not coming from there. Besides that point, do you really think the average believer is going to look at a prophecy from an unbeliever with a lot of sincerity? We know from the Old Testament accounts that false prophets can be in what we would call the church. So unless something really changes in the world's scene, my conclusion is that these false prophets who will deceive many people is happening in the church.

Again, why will this get into the church? Let me quote one of the scriptures I have listed above: "For the time will come when men will not put up with sound doctrine. Instead, to suit their own desires, they will gather around them a great number of teachers to say *what their itching ears want to hear*. They will turn their ears away from the truth and turn aside to myths" (2 Tm 4:3–4, niv).

For too many people, the last days will not be a time where they are sincerely searching for truth. It will be a time that is built around selfishness. People will be looking for ministers who agree with them on what they believe and tell them what they want to hear. This is going to severely hamper the convincing/conviction of the Holy Spirit (John 16:7–11). Again we see the anointing of the Holy Spirit being quenched. And what is quenching it? Selfishness. It's the attitude of "I am only going to listen to what I want to hear."

Back to Matthew 24:

Verse 12. *Wickedness* (G458, *Strong's*)

"From 459; illegality, that is, violation of law or (generally) wickedness. :—iniquity, X transgress (-ion of) the law, unrighteousness."

(G459–Strong's) Defined as: "lawless, i.e. not subject to law".

As *iniquity* (kjv) or *wickedness* (niv) or *lawlessness* (amp) increases, the love for God (and/or love for fellow human beings) will get less and less.

This characteristic of wickedness—or lawlessness—will be looked at more deeply in the next chapter. *Lawlessness is tied directly to selfishness.*

Verse 13. Our command is to stand firm in Jesus until this whole thing is over.

Verse 38. The people will be living life as usual (viewing life as being "normal"). Nothing will stand out as unusual. That is a true indicator of deception. *Without the Holy Spirit's help, we cannot see where we are deceived. Everything will look normal to us. This is the condition of the last-day society. Even though there are clear indications that there is a huge problem, people will still think and feel like everything is fine.* Again I say it, that is a result of deception.

Verse 39. Therefore, they were oblivious to what was happening around them and what was about to happen on the earth.

The book of Mark adds a few details to this:

> 9 You must be on your guard. You will be handed over to the local councils and flogged in the synagogues. On account of me you will stand before governors and kings as witnesses to them. 10 And the gospel must first be preached to all nations. 12

> Brother will betray brother to death, and a father his child. Children will rebel against their parents and have them put to death. 13 All men will hate you because of me, but he who stands firm to the end will be saved. (Mk 13:9–10, 12–13, niv)

Verse 9. Not only are we to "watch," but we need to "be on guard." There will be increased persecution from all levels of government ("local councils; governors and kings), as well as increased persecution from the established religious arena ("synagogues") because of a person's stance on Jesus and his word. This is going to be used as a witness to them. Nevertheless, there will be increased governmental and religious pressure.

Verse 12. This persecution will infest families. Children and parents will betray each other.

Verse 13. The core of the problem—Jesus. Anyone who takes a stand for Jesus will be made a target.

As believers, our focus and job will be to "stand firm" until it's all over.

Presuming Jesus knew what he was talking about here—and I would think we are safe in presuming that—the increase of public sentiment against God, Jesus, the Bible, etc. is going to continue to grow until it gets quite wicked. It will rip families, churches, denominations, and governments apart. It will cause hate to grow against anyone who takes a stand for Jesus and godliness.

Notice that in Luke 18, Jesus expresses his concern for how much faith will still be around when he returns.

> 1 Then Jesus told his disciples a parable to show them that they should always pray and not give up. 2 He said: "In a certain town there was a judge who neither feared God nor cared about men. 3 And there was a widow in that town who kept coming to him with the plea, 'Grant me justice against my adversary.' 4 For some time he refused. But finally he said to himself, 'Even though I don't fear God or care about men, 5 yet because this widow keeps bothering me, I will see that she gets justice, so that she won't eventually wear me out with her coming!'" 6 And the Lord said, "Listen to what the unjust judge says. 7 And will not God bring about justice for his chosen ones, who cry out to him day and night? Will he keep putting them off? 8 I tell you, he will see that they get justice, and quickly. *However, when the Son of Man comes, will he find faith on the earth?*" (Lk 18:1–8, niv)

The same question can be asked right here: how did the church ever get to this point? How did Christians slide so far in the wrong direction that Jesus is concerned about how much faith He will actually find when He returns?

That's simple: instead of being an unmovable force of restraint (2 Thessalonians 2:6), too many believers lost their saltiness and hid their light (Matthew 5:13–16). As a result, instead of us influencing the people of this world to become like Jesus, we submitted to their influence and became what the Antichrist spirit was trying to form in us. We are consumed with our own interests, desires, goals, plans, pleasures, and entertainment. We will do whatever it takes to put ourselves, our family, our interests, and pretty much anything that affects our life and comfort in the position of being first. Whatever benefits us the most is what the average believer will choose. And if it doesn't benefit us in some way, the average person isn't interested. Bottom line—we're selfish.

I realize putting it that way will probably shock some people, and of course our first instinct is to deny and say we are nothing like Satan or the Antichrist spirit. I would love to quickly agree with that. But we must measure against the

> Instead of us influencing the people of this world to become like Jesus, we submitted to their influence and became what the Antichrist spirit was trying to form in us.

kind of fruit that is coming from our lives. If it's not righteousness or like God, then there's only one other being that we are like—Satan. There's nothing in scripture to indicate there are three choices: God, us, and Satan. Everything flows back to two sources: the kingdom of God or the kingdom of the devil. Look at what John said in 1

John chapter 3 (We covered it in ch. 1 of this book). Our 'righteous' or 'unrighteous' behavior is a clear indicator which spirit is influencing us the most. If it's the Spirit of God, our behavior will be righteous. If it's the spirit of Antichrist, our behavior will be unrighteous.

So why will Christians find themselves in such a disgusting situation in the last days? It is because we will be overcome with the breath of the anti-anointing (spirit of Antichrist). And what did it produce in us? It produced the ground that grows everything from the kingdom of darkness. It produced a group of people who are very selfish.

There's one more large section of scripture that we need to look at to see the characteristics that will be in the church in the last days. It's found in the book of Revelation: the seven churches of Revelation.

It is usually thought that only the Laodicean church is giving characteristics of what the last-day church will be like. However, I don't think that is true. When you look at all the churches and the negative characteristics that Jesus said needed improving, they go hand in hand with the other scriptures that tell us what the last-day society will be like. What happened? The characteristics of a godless society crept into the church. As we look at these seven churches, I think you'll agree that Jesus was addressing characteristics that are alive, well, and gaining influence in the church today. For that reason, I think all of the seven churches are depicting the condition of the church in the last day.

Because of that, I have listed the scriptures concerning the seven churches in Revelation.

I want to be sure that you notice something. In every church, Jesus points out things they are doing correctly. He commends them for what they're doing right. So please notice this: it's not the things we are doing right that cause us our problems; it's the things we are doing wrong. If these things are allowed to remain, they will eventually spoil what we're doing right (1 Corinthians 5:6; 15:33).

Also please notice: the Holy Spirit is actively at work and trying to emphasize something in every church. The Spirit will be speaking to the last-day church! The question is will we be listening and obedient? That's why it's repeated over and over: "He who has and ear, let him hear what the Spirit says to the churches."

Five of the seven churches had issues that needed to be addressed and cleaned up. In two of the churches, Jesus did not point out anything that needed correction. I call these the *bride* or *remnant* churches. They were without spot, wrinkle, or blemish and were holy and blameless (Eph. 5:27). However, the majority—five churches—had things for which they needed to repent and fix. These are the characteristics of what is going to try to get in or is going to be in to the last-day church. We'll look at them, one church at a time.

> 1 To the angel of the church in Ephesus write: These are the words of him who holds the seven stars in his right hand and walks among the seven golden

lampstands: 2 I know your deeds, your hard work and your perseverance. I know that you cannot tolerate wicked men, that you have tested those who claim to be apostles but are not, and have found them false. 3 You have persevered and have endured hardships for my name, and have not grown weary. 4 Yet I hold this against you: *You have forsaken your first love.* 5 Remember the height from which you have fallen! Repent and do the things you did at first. If you do not repent, I will come to you and remove your lampstand from its place. 6 But you have this in your favor: You hate the practices of the Nicolaitans, which I also hate. 7 He who has an ear, let him hear what the Spirit says to the churches. To him who overcomes, I will give the right to eat from the tree of life, which is in the paradise of God. (Rev 2:1–7, niv; emphasis added)

Characteristics

Though this church was doing some awesome things, Jesus was no longer their first love. If Jesus wasn't first, then who was? My guess is this: they were looking out for their own interests first. That's the way our old nature does it. Unless we are intentionally looking out for the interests of someone else before our own, we will gravitate to taking care of what we want first. It's called *selfishness* (compare 2 Timothy 3:2). Their passion, zeal, intensity, and commitment to Jesus had waned and grown cool. Jesus was personally holding that against them as an issue with which they had to deal.

> 8 To the angel of the church in Smyrna write: (Remnant, or Bride Church) These are the words of him who is the First and the Last, who died and came to life again. 9 I know your afflictions and your poverty—yet you are rich! I know the slander of those who say they are Jews and are not, but are a synagogue of Satan. 10 Do not be afraid of what you are about to suffer. I tell you, the devil will put some of you in prison to test you, and you will suffer persecution for ten days. Be faithful, even to the point of death, and I will give you the crown of life. 11 He who has an ear, let him hear what the Spirit says to the churches. He who overcomes will not be hurt at all by the second death. (Rev 2:8–11, niv)

Characteristics

Jesus had nothing negative to say about this church. How they were pursuing Him was great. This is an example of the type of believers we are to be. It is possible to live our life in such a way that Jesus has nothing negative to say about it. It is possible to be holy and blameless (Eph. 5:27). He addresses the fact they are facing physical afflictions and poverty, attacks from the devil and prison. Religious people are slandering them. They will face some suffering, but they are not to fear. Jesus encourages them to remain faithful even if it costs them their life. They need to overcome so they won't be hurt by the second death. So it's not that they are having it easy and without opposition, but they are walking it out in such a way that Jesus has nothing negative to say about them.

> 12 To the angel of the church in Pergamum write: These are the words of him who has the sharp, double-edged sword. 13 I know where you live—where Satan has his throne. Yet you remain true to my name. You did not renounce your faith in me, even in the days of Antipas, my faithful witness, who was put to death in your city—where Satan lives. 14 *Nevertheless, I have a few things against you: You have people there who hold to the teaching of Balaam, who taught Balak to entice the Israelites to sin by eating food sacrificed to idols and by committing sexual immorality.* 15 Likewise *you also have those who hold to the teaching of the Nicolaitans.* 16 *Repent therefore! Otherwise, I will soon come to you and will fight against them with the sword of my mouth.* 17 He who has an ear, let him hear what the Spirit says to the churches. To him who overcomes, I will give some of the hidden manna. I will also give him a white stone with a new name written on it, known only to him who receives it. (Rev 2:12–17, niv; emphasis added)

Characteristics

This church was located in a very difficult area spiritually. Satan had his throne there. What does that tell us? From Jesus's perspective, the degradation of the area we live in shouldn't have anything to do with how we live out our Christian life. We should be overcomers no matter what the society or environment we live in is like. We find a few things mentioned here that Jesus was not happy with. Let's look at the Balaam issue first. (The entire story of Balaam is found in Numbers 22:1–24:25.)

Balaam is referred to three times in the New Testament (2 Peter 2:15, Jude 11, Revelation 2:14). Each of the New Testament references are giving some insight into the mindset of Balaam. So we'll look at all three of them to see if we can find what the teaching of Balaam would have been.

"They have left the straight way and wandered off to follow the way of Balaam son of Beor, who *loved the wages of wickedness*. But he was rebuked for his wrongdoing by a donkey—a beast without speech—who spoke with a man's voice and restrained the prophet's madness" (2 Pet. 2:15–16, niv; emphasis added).

The word *wages* here is referring to silver and gold in the original language (money). God had already told Balaam what he should do, but when he was promised the honor of wealth, he had problems resisting. He was lured by the wages. Balaam's problem was that he put more importance on money than what God had told him to do. (Compare 2 Timothy 3:2. The same thing happens in the last days.)

"Woe to them! For they have run riotously in the way of Cain, and have *abandoned themselves for the sake of gain [it offers them, following] the error of Balaam*, and have perished in rebellion [like that] of Korah! [Gen. 4:3–8, Num. 16, 22–24]" (Jude 11, amp; emphasis added).

Again, it's telling us the same thing as 2 Peter 2:15. There is too much importance being placed on money or financial wealth. People are abandoning the more important priorities in life for financial gain (more money). Money and finances are a huge driving force in this. Jesus said you can't serve both God and money (Matt. 6:24). The lure of money and finances can draw a person into numerous pursuits with which God does not agree. That's how I think the principles of 2 Peter 2:15 and Jude 11 play into this picture. Balaam was drawn into pursuits in which he shouldn't have been involved. He did it, and we can follow suit because of a desire for more money, nice things, a new house, cars, etc., the things money can get for us. It becomes more about what we want than what God wants (selfishness). *This is going to be a dominating characteristic to prove the Antichrist spirit is resting on a person. The emphasis of gaining money and wealth will take precedence over doing God's will in a person's life. (Just like it did with Balaam.)*

In Revelation 2:14 it goes on to say: "Nevertheless, I have a few things against you: You have people there who hold to the teaching of Balaam, who taught Balak *to entice the Israelites to sin by eating food sacrificed to idols and by committing sexual immorality*" (Rev. 2:14, niv; emphasis added).

Here it specifically mentions two things:

1. eating food sacrificed to idols and
2. committing sexual immorality.

Let's look at number 1, food being sacrificed to idols. Paul talks about this subject quite a bit. Here's one of the key passages where Paul talks about it.

> 14 Therefore, my dear friends, flee from idolatry. 15 I speak to sensible people; judge for yourselves what I say. 16 Is not the cup of thanksgiving for which we give thanks a participation in the blood of Christ? And is not the bread that we break a participation in the body of Christ? 17 Because there is one loaf, we, who are many, are one body, for we all partake of the one loaf. 18 *Consider the people of Israel: Do not those who eat the sacrifices participate in the altar?* 19 Do I mean then that a sacrifice offered to an idol is anything, or that an idol is anything? 20 No, but *the sacrifices of pagans are offered to demons, not to God, and I do not want you to be participants with demons. 21 You cannot drink the cup of the Lord and the cup of demons too; you cannot have a part in both the Lord's table and the table of demons.* 22 Are we trying to

> arouse the Lord's jealousy? Are we stronger than he? 23 "Everything is permissible"—but not everything is beneficial. "Everything is permissible"—but not everything is constructive. 24 *Nobody should seek his own good, but the good of others.* 25 Eat anything sold in the meat market without raising questions of conscience, 26 for, "The earth is the Lord's, and everything in it." 27 If some unbeliever invites you to a meal and you want to go, eat whatever is put before you without raising questions of conscience. 28 But if anyone says to you, "This has been offered in sacrifice," then do not eat it, both for the sake of the man who told you and for conscience' sake—29 the other man's conscience, I mean, not yours. For why should my freedom be judged by another's conscience? 30 If I take part in the meal with thankfulness, why am I denounced because of something I thank God for? 31 *So whether you eat or drink or whatever you do, do it all for the glory of God. 32 Do not cause anyone to stumble, whether Jews, Greeks or the church of God*—33 *even as I try to please everybody in every way. For I am not seeking my own good but the good of many, so that they may be saved.* 1 Follow my example, as I follow the example of Christ. (1 Cor 10:14–11:1, niv; emphasis added)

His conclusion for New Testament people is that the *physical* eating of food that had been sacrificed to idols wasn't a big deal (1 Corinthians 10:19–20a). However there are two things he points out that *are* a big deal.

The Breath of Anti-Christ

First of all (verses 14–22), don't get involved with things that are intentionally designed to further demonic purposes. When we do, Paul says we are "participants with demons." What kinds of things is Paul talking about? To answer that, ask yourself this question: whose cause is it furthering, God's or the devil's? Take a look at every activity of your life and everything you do in life. Are they designed to further the Kingdom of Darkness? If you measure them against what is right or Godly, how do they measure up? I say it that way because too often Christians say: I don't see anything wrong with doing _____ (you fill in the blank). Since when should our measure of righteousness be against how "wrong" something is? We should be measuring against how "right" something is! If a person is being led into sin by participating with some activity, Paul says we are participating with demons. As Christians we shouldn't be "drinking of the Lord's cup, and the cup of demons too." So even though, from our perspective, the thing we are doing may not be currently harming us or be a problem to us (v. 23–it's permissible but because of the spiritual context, it's not beneficial), the real problem is that we are submitting to and embracing the wrong spiritual force/kingdom (demons). In the Corinthians situation, it was eating food that had been sacrificed to idols. In Paul's mind, not only was it not beneficial, this was something very serious. He compared it to taking communion (the blood and body of Jesus). He's saying don't take communion with demons by getting involved with what they do.

Verse 23 is typically the verse used by believers to say that they can do their own thing. In context, that's not really what Paul is saying. But let's say for a moment that Paul is giving us permission to do whatever we want. My question is this: even in that case, why would we want to do something that is not beneficial or constructive to our life as a Christian or other peoples' Christian lives? The only answer I've ever received from anyone who has that viewpoint is that's talking about weaker Christians. They can handle it. So listen closely to what was just said in that statement: I want to do this so I'm going to.

What do you hear in that? Selfishness. It's all about me. It's a very selfish mindset and belief system.

Please notice that evidently Paul had people telling him the same kinds of things, and he too saw the core of the problem. He points out in verses 24 and 33: we are not to be seeking our own good. Or in other words, we're not supposed to be selfish in our choices. In verses 14–22, Paul is talking about pleasing God. In verse 23–24, Paul is talking about loving other people. Do you remember reading something like that in another scripture? Hint: the two greatest commandments (Matthew 22:37–40). So again, it comes back to the question of who are we going to love more: God, via the two greatest commands, or ourselves by doing what we want to do, selfishness. (Compare 2 Timothy 3:2.)

The second principle Paul points out in this section of scripture is this: everything we do is not about us, but it needs to be about the purpose of getting other people saved (v. 24–33). That really strikes at the heart of selfishness. This section of scripture—food being sacrificed to idols— is actually dealing with how self-centered/self-seeking we're going to be in our relationship with Jesus, as well as how self-centered/self-seeking we are going to be in regard to reaching the lost. Are we going to be selfish and make our life all about ourselves? Or are we going to drop the selfishness and make our lives about God and what He wants to happen in other people?

What's the application for us? We are living in a society that is enamored with things that lead people into sin. They don't point us toward Jesus, but rather they pull us away from Him. Jesus said anything that is not for Him is against Him (Matt. 12:30). There are only two sides to this war. We must pay close attention to what we allow ourselves be involved. Many things in this world do not produce Godly fruit. We shouldn't be involved with them. However, like in five of the seven churches in the book of Revelation chapters 2–3, Christians will be involved in all kinds of things that do not promote God's kingdom but the devil's kingdom. That is how we are participating with demons and literally are in communion/agreement with them.

This will be a trait of the End Times. The church will make excuses for beliefs, priorities, and actions that are ungodly. Since these things won't be spoken against or pointed out as things of which we need to get out of our lives, they will make their way into the church. In reality, the church will be promoting the Antichrist agenda by allowing people to hold on to beliefs and lifestyles that are obviously ungodly (five of the churches of Rev. chapters 2–3).

There is the first thing that Jesus had a problem with in the church of Pergamum (food sacrificed to idols). Now let's go to the second thing with which Jesus was taking issue.

Number 2, committing sexual immorality. In Rev. 2:14, it says that Balaam taught Balak to offer his women to the Israelite men (the result of this is referred to in Numbers 25:1–9). We don't know the exact circumstances surrounding this, but the thing that Jesus points out in Rev. 2:14 is sexual immorality. Balaam knew if the Israelites became involved in sexual immorality, God would get angry with them and possibly curse them Himself (Numbers 31:14–16). The result would be that the Israelites would come under a curse, and Balaam would not have done it. And that's exactly what happened. God became angry, and many were killed for their sin (Num. 25:1–9).

Here's the application for us. An ever-increasing trait of our time is sexual immorality. It is common for Christians to have sex outside of marriage. It is becoming common for believers to live together before they're married. The whole politically correct thing of "tolerance" is quickly making inroads into the church. Many churches and believers are accepting the homosexual and lesbian lifestyle as normal. In reality, these things are condemned in the New Testament as an alternative behavior. These things are sin. They do not bring the blessing but open us to a curse. They can be repented of, and the blessing of God again returns, but they are not to be accepted as normal. We are not to view them as "well that's how society is now. It's a different world than it used to be." This is a trait in the church that is becoming prevalent. Why? It is being pushed by the spirit of Antichrist. And why are Christians buying into the myth that these things are okay with God? Because somehow that works out better for them. It allows them to have the lifestyle they want. It may diminish any repercussions that could take place in families. Plus, if there are any physical or emotional irregularities, it releases them from pursuing health while still giving legitimacy to the lifestyle. It's convenient, easy, and self-serving. It is very much active in the church right now. It is an area where the Antichrist spirit is making huge inroads into the church.

Now let's look at the teaching of the Nicolaitans.

> These were the followers of Nicolaus, a heretic. They are supposed to have been a sect of gnostics who practiced and taught impure and immoral doctrines—such as the community of wives—and that committing adultery and fornication was not sinful. This was similar to the doctrines of Balaam and Jezebel of Thyatira. (Rev. 2:6, 14–15, 20)

Source: *Dake's Annotated Bible*.

Before we discuss gnosticism, ask yourself this question: what causes a person to commit adultery, fornication, or want multiple wives? Push that question deep enough and you will likely find selfishness.

Gnosticism is going to be a problem among Christians. It is the backdrop to what the apostle John was dealing with in the book of First John when he was addressing the issues surrounding the power of Antichrist. Gnosticism can be summed up with one word—*knowledge*. Since gnosticism is tied to the word *gnosis*, which means, "knowledge of spiritual mysteries," it is all about knowing things of God or true spirituality that other people don't know. Gnostics feel they have a revelation or higher knowledge about God that the average Christian does not have. The sect began in the second century. It continues to rear its ugly head about various doctrines and issues throughout Christianity. One of the most recent issues we have been dealing with in our time is *hypergrace*. Gnosticism *is* touching and *will* touch many other doctrines and beliefs. It is an ongoing problem because there is always someone who feels they've been shown something and have a knowledge that the average Christian does not have. Because of this superior knowledge and revelation, they know secrets and mysteries about God and the spirit realm that are beyond most believers. It becomes the basis for much of their thinking, attitudes, and behaviors. Typically, it is steeped in some form of error and does not agree with the full counsel of the scripture. Interestingly, it becomes a way of thinking that is very self-serving (selfish). Gnosticism is also a characteristic of the last days.

In verse 16, Jesus gives a stern warning. He says repent of this, or I will come and fight against those who are promoting these things. It is possible for Jesus to take a stand against what is happening in a church. That's a scary thought! Jesus fighting against people in the church! What if the people He's opposing are in leadership or maybe even the pastors? Now, there will be definite spiritual problems in that church until they repent. The point is we must pay attention to what we are doing and whether Jesus/the Holy Spirit are happy with it. Jesus isn't happy with everything that happens in church. And depending on what it is, rather than help the church, we will find Him fighting against us. And the tool He uses to fight with is the sword of His mouth. That in itself should be sobering. There are a number of places it refers to a sword in regard to Jesus (Ephesians 6:17; Hebrews 4:12). However, the sword of the mouth is only found in the book of Revelation. Here are the references:

> In his right hand He held seven stars, *and out of His mouth came a sharp double-edged sword.* His face was like the sun shining in all its brilliance. (Rev. 1:16, niv; emphasis added)

> To the angel of the church in Pergamum write: *These are the words of Him who has the sharp, double-edged sword.* Repent therefore! Otherwise, I will soon come to you and will *fight against them with the sword of my mouth.* (Rev. 2:12, 16, niv; emphasis added)
>
> *Out of his mouth comes a sharp sword with which to strike down the nations. "He will rule them with an iron scepter." He treads the winepress of the fury of the wrath of God Almighty. The rest of them were killed with the sword that came out of the mouth of the rider on the horse, and all the birds gorged themselves on their flesh. (Rev. 19:15, 21, niv; emphasis added)*

The first couple of references are stating that Jesus has a sword coming out of his mouth. Then in chapter 2 verse 16 and chapter 19 verses 15 and 21, it tells us what the sword is used for. I'll sum it up by saying no matter how you look at it, when Jesus uses the sword of his mouth against someone or a nation, it is not going to turn out well for them.

Again Jesus ends what he has to say to Pergamum with an encouragement to pay attention to the Holy Spirit. Here the Spirit is saying that we may have some things to overcome, but that we should do it because of the rewards that will be given to the overcomer.

> 18 To the angel of the church in Thyatira write: These are the words of the Son of God, whose eyes are like blazing fire and whose feet are like burnished bronze. 19 I know your deeds, your love and faith,

your service and perseverance, and that you are now doing more than you did at first. 20 *Nevertheless, I have this against you: You tolerate that woman Jezebel,* who calls herself a prophetess. *By her teaching she misleads my servants into sexual immorality and the eating of food sacrificed to idols.* 21 I have given her time to repent of her immorality, but she is unwilling. 22 So I will cast her on a bed of suffering, and I will make those who commit adultery with her suffer intensely, unless they repent of her ways. 23 I will strike her children dead. Then all the churches will know that I am he who searches hearts and minds, and I will repay each of you according to your deeds. 24 Now I say to the rest of you in Thyatira, to you who do not hold to her teaching and have not learned Satan's so-called deep secrets (I will not impose any other burden on you): 25 Only hold on to what you have until I come. 26 To him who overcomes and does my will to the end, I will give authority over the nations—27 "He will rule them with an iron scepter; he will dash them to pieces like pottery"—just as I have received authority from my Father. 28 I will also give him the morning star. 29 He who has an ear, let him hear what the Spirit says to the churches. (Rev. 2:18–29; emphasis added)

Characteristics

See the notes on Nicolaitans under the church of Pergamum (above). Again, notice the same three things as with the church of Pergamum: sexual immorality, food sacrificed to idols, and gnosticism (1) "her teaching" (v. 20), and (2) "Satan's so-called deep secrets" (v. 24).

In speaking to this church, Jesus adds one more dimension to these three. He says that he holds it against them that they are tolerating the woman Jezebel. There is a point at which "tolerance" of others—via allowing them to be part of the group and influence with their line of thinking—is not acceptable to God. Since the church did not remove her, Jesus will. If she and her followers repent, everything can change. If not, there will be consequences. I realize there are many teachings on Jezebel and the type of spiritual influence that accompanied her. I'm not going to touch any of those things in this book. The reason is because Jesus specifically named the influences she was having in the church at Thyatira. Those are the characteristics I want to focus on: her teaching, sexual immorality, and food sacrificed to idols.

Since Jesus had issue with her "teaching," it would be safe to assume that she also had some form of higher revelation than merely the Bible (Gnosticism), and was basing her teaching on the higher revelations ("Satan's so-called deep secrets")— and not the Bible. That's how she could lead people into sexual immorality and food sacrifice to idols, and still present it as they were serving God. It would also make sense with the statement Jesus made about her calling herself a prophetess. This is also an issue in Jesus's mind. I am not belittling the fact that the Bible does say prophets will play an important role in the last days. But I will say this: If a prophet gives some form of revelation that contradicts the written word of God, (the Bible) DO NOT PAY ANY ATTENTION TO WHAT THEY HAVE TO SAY. Obviously, Jezebel's higher revelations of teaching were also accompanied by her being a prophet. As strongly as the Godly prophetic office is needed in the last days, let me say there are a lot of weird and unscriptural people running around claiming to be speaking for God, having a higher or new revelation, and are leading people astray. (Just like Jezebel) This is going to be a significant problem in the last days' church. How do we know what to believe, and what to throw away? IF IT DOES NOT AGREE WITH THE WRITTEN WORD OF GOD (The Bible), THROW IT AWAY. IT'S GARBAGE.

I will not cover the three things listed above again. They have already been explained under the characteristics of the previous church—Pergamum.

However, I do want you to notice a couple of similarities between Pergamum and Thyatira. First of all, they are both struggling with similar issues. Secondly, Jesus comes and personally deals with them. In Thyatira, we have an enlargement on how Jesus can deal with churches. Even though the sword of his mouth is not mentioned to Thyatira, I believe it's referring to the same thing because of how he deals with them. It also gives us some insight into what can happen when Jesus comes and deals with sinful things in a church. In verse 22–23, we see "suffering, death, and repayment according to deeds / works." If this is the discipline we read of in Hebrews 12, it is pretty intense. No matter how you look at it, it does appear to be some form of judgment. It is similar to what Paul told the Corinthians regarding taking communion incorrectly (1 Corinthians 11:27–32, niv and amp). It has to do with a judgment and discipline that is focused on the redemption of the person. That's the same thing he told the church of Thyatira about the woman called Jezebel. He was doing this so she would repent (v. 21–22).

Now we are seeing a trend develop. When things are happening in the church that are causing it to become unrighteous, first of all, Jesus expects the church to do something about it; and secondly, if the church doesn't step up to deal with it, He will. We saw this in Ephesus (Rev. 2:5). We also saw it in Pergamum (Rev. 2:16). We are seeing it in Thyatira (Rev. 2:21–23). You will see the same thing in the other two churches that Jesus rebukes, Sardis (Rev. 3:3) and Laodicea (Rev. 3:16).

Jesus loves the church (*ekklesia* in the Greek. It's talking about the people who have been called out of the kingdom of darkness and have formed into a congregation) very much. But He will allow it to go only so far into demise before He will come to rebuke and discipline it. So it is safe to say that what Jesus is telling us via these churches is that He will actively be involved with the church of the last days. Should they remain in line with his Spirit, they will be commended. Should they stray, they will be dealt with accordingly. Some churches will remain and grow strong in the things of the Spirit. Others will be rebuked, disciplined, and as in one case, have their candlestick removed (Ephesus in chapter 2 verse 5). Or to say it another way, they'll have their official status as a Church of Jesus removed. Their doors may stay open. People may still come. But as far as Jesus is concerned, they are not a church.

How will we know which church is doing well and which one is struggling? Jesus tells us. He made the same statement to all seven churches: "He who has an ear, let him hear what the Spirit says to the churches." He says it in chapter 2 verses 7, 11, 17, 29, and chapter 3 verses 6, 13, 22.

The Holy Spirit will be very actively trying to speak to all of the last-day churches. We are admonished to listen (pay attention). Here's the big question: is the Holy Spirit speaking to your church? If so, what is He saying? How do you know He's speaking to the people, the congregation? Is there clear evidence that He's not only speaking, but that the leadership and the people are listening?

Why is that important? Because the indication of these seven churches is that most last-day churches will not be listening to what the Spirit is saying. The proof of that is they will be having all kinds of things happening in their congregation that are clearly not God. And it will be tolerated and even presented as acceptable. The Holy Spirit would never agree with that. He will be trying to cleanse the church of these types of things. So the more carnal, ungodly, and filled with the mind-set of the world a church is, the more clearly the church is not being led by the Spirit and is likely in trouble with the Master of the church—Jesus Christ.

The last thing I want to mention about the church of Thyatira is found in verses 26–28. Again, it is similar to the church of Pergamum. He talks about rewards for overcoming. The difference is that to Thyatira, he lists some of the rewards. He lists, "authority over nations, rulership, and the morning star" being given as rewards. I don't think anyone fully knows what that all means, but of this much we can be sure *it's going to be awesome!*

So again let's heed the admonition from Jesus: *"He who has an ear, let him hear what the Spirit says to the churches."*

> 1 To the angel of the church in Sardis write: These are the words of him who holds the seven spirits of God and the seven stars. I know your deeds; you have a reputation of being alive, but *you are dead.* 2 Wake up! Strengthen what remains and is about to die, for I have not found your deeds complete in the sight of my God. 3 Remember, therefore, what you have received and heard; obey it, and repent. But if you do not wake up, I will come like a thief, and you will not know at what time I will come to you. 4 Yet you have a few people in Sardis who have not soiled their clothes. They will walk with me, dressed in white, for they are worthy. 5 He who overcomes will, like them, be dressed in white. I will

never blot out his name from the book of life, but
will acknowledge his name before my Father and his
angels. 6 He who has an ear, let him hear what the
Spirit says to the churches. (Rev. 3:1–6, niv;
emphasis added)

Characteristics

Verse 1. By their works/deeds, Jesus can tell they are not spiritually alive, but rather He considered them spiritually dead. What are the deeds that Jesus was looking at? He didn't say, so we don't know. But this much we can say with certainty: what we do as Christians matters! Jesus is watching our deeds/works. And he can tell if we are "alive" or "dead" spiritually simply by watching what we do. A good question for us to ask here would go something like: Are the things I do in my life evidence of a God who is living inside me and leading me by his Spirit? Or are they evidence that I am making my own decisions and living life in the manner I choose? (Selfishness) Because according to John 15:1–8, any good fruit that comes from our life can only come via staying connected with God. This is important because Godly fruit can only be produced where there is Godly 'life" and the person has be made "alive."

Verse 2. I find it interesting that Jesus refers to their "deeds" or "works" two times. And it's the deeds/works He's looking at that show Him they are dead spiritually. Deeds/works are to flow from our lives as believers. God is looking at our deeds/works. When we have true faith, there will be deeds/works that will accompany it (cf. James 2:17). According to how the church of Sardis is living, they have become so self-serving that they are quickly losing any spiritual life they may have left. They have deeds/works, but they aren't the kind Jesus is looking for.

Verses 2–3. He tells us what He is looking for. They are sleeping spiritually. They need to "wake up." They need to remember what they have already received and heard and start living it (obey). If they don't wake up, there will be consequences.

Verse 4–5. Again, Jesus states there are some who are doing well. He also gives more understanding to the rewards that will be given to the overcomer. He lists several reward items: "walk with Him, dressed in white, never blotted out of the book of life, acknowledge their name before the Father and his Angels."

Verse 6. So listen to what the Spirit is saying.

> 7 To the angel of the church in Philadelphia write: (Remnant, or Bride Church). These are the words of him who is holy and true, who holds the key of David. What he opens no one can shut, and what he shuts no one can open. 8 I know your deeds. See, I have placed before you an open door that no one can shut. I know that you have little strength, yet you have kept my word and have not denied my name. 9 I will make those who are of the synagogue

of Satan, who claim to be Jews though they are not, but are liars—I will make them come and fall down at your feet and acknowledge that I have loved you. 10 Since you have kept my command to endure patiently, I will also keep you from the hour of trial that is going to come upon the whole world to test those who live on the earth. 11 I am coming soon. Hold on to what you have, so that no one will take your crown. 12 Him who overcomes I will make a pillar in the temple of my God. Never again will he leave it. I will write on him the name of my God and the name of the city of my God, the new Jerusalem, which is coming down out of heaven from my God; and I will also write on him my new name. 13 He who has an ear, let him hear what the Spirit says to the churches. (Rev. 3:7–13, niv)

Characteristics

Jesus had nothing negative to say. This is our goal. To live for Jesus with such diligence and sincerity that He will have nothing negative to say about us. Again, many rewards are listed for living this life out in the manner Jesus desires.

> 14 To the angel of the church in Laodicea write: These are the words of the Amen, the faithful and true witness, the ruler of God's creation. 15 I know your deeds, that *you are neither cold nor hot*. I wish you were either one or the other! 16 So, because *you are lukewarm—neither hot nor cold*—I am about to spit

you out of my mouth. 17 You say, "I am rich; I have acquired wealth and do not need a thing." But *you do not realize that you are wretched, pitiful, poor, blind and naked.* 18 I counsel you to buy from me gold refined in the fire, so you can become rich; and white clothes to wear, so you can cover your shameful nakedness; and salve to put on your eyes, so you can see. 19 Those whom I love I rebuke and discipline. So be earnest, and repent. 20 Here I am! I stand at the door and knock. If anyone hears my voice and opens the door, I will come in and eat with him, and he with me. 21 To him who overcomes, I will give the right to sit with me on my throne, just as I overcame and sat down with my Father on his throne. 22 He who has an ear, let him hear what the Spirit says to the churches. (Rev. 3:14–22, niv; emphasis added)

Characteristics

In Jesus's opinion, they are lukewarm spiritually. They are wretched, pitiful, poor, blind, and naked. Yet in their opinion, they are saying they are doing very well. They are basing this on their money and financial prosperity. In the western world, this has become a huge problem in the church. If we are doing well financially, then we feel we are doing well spiritually. In reality, that may be the furthest thing from the truth. Paul warns about tying financial gain and Godliness together in our mind (1 Timothy 6:5b). This issue of the wrong emphasis on money and finances has now shown up in two churches: Pergamum and Laodicea. In the last days, measuring our spiritual condition by our financial wealth and prosperity is going to be a big problem in the church.

Interestingly, while they were measuring themselves by the material realm, Jesus is looking at their spiritual condition, and it is very bleak (v. 17b). They are looking at their physical condition (finances and wealth) and are using it as the standard of how well they are doing spiritually. They say, "I am rich and do not need a thing." They are all about themselves (selfish).

In reality, we cannot measure our spiritual condition by our financial condition. If that were the case, some of the most wealthy people on the face of the earth would have to be considered Godly. In fact, many don't even serve Jesus but serve a different god.

Again, notice the emphasis Jesus placed on "deeds/works" (v. 15). Their deeds were telling Jesus that these people were lukewarm spiritually. They were satisfied, comfortable, financially doing well, and felt like they were doing fine ("do not need a thing" [v. 17]). He also talked about discipline, rebuke, and repentance (v. 19). In verse 21, He lists a huge reward for overcoming: sitting on His throne (rulership and dominion will be given to the overcomers).

As we have just seen, there is a huge amount of information concerning the last days and the condition of society, and specifically the church in the book of Revelation. Again, it's painting a picture that gives many characteristics of what the Antichrist spirit is trying to accomplish in believers, literally listing the things we must pay attention to and overcome.

Here is another scripture that gives the spiritual condition of the church in the last days: "For the time will come when *men will not put up with sound doctrine. Instead, to suit their own desires, they will gather* around them a great number of *teachers to say what their itching ears want to hear. They will turn their ears away from the truth and turn aside to myths*" (2 Tim. 4:3–4, niv; emphasis added).

These two verses actually have a lot to show us concerning the church in the days before Jesus returns. What Paul is warning about is happening in the church right now, and it will continue to grow in momentum. Sound doctrine—or what the Bible has to say—is no longer the final authority or basis for what is believed and taught in many churches and denominations. Why? Because people don't like what the Bible says. Plus, many Christians question whether the Bible is actually the word of God or simply a book of stories that talks about history. As a result, they look for churches and ministers who will say what they want to hear even though it's not what the scripture is saying. Believers will intentionally "turn their ears away from hearing the truth and turn aside to myths."

That is horrible. How can the church have gotten to this point? Paul gives us the answer. He tells us two times what the motivator for this deception will be. The people will want doctrine and teachers who will "suit their own desires"—"what their itching ears want to hear." What is he describing? Selfishness.

As a minister, here is the really sad and scary part to me. There will be a great number of these teachers and ministers who are willing to say things to simply get a crowd. The scripture says "they will gather around them a great number of teachers" who will say things that, according to verse 4, are not the truth, but in reality are myths. *What happened to the men and women of God–the ministers–who are willing to take a stand for the truth no matter how many people will or won't listen? We as ministers are as much to blame as anyone else!* We should be proclaiming the truth, but instead a "great number" of us will have turned to and embraced error. The result: the huge deception is propagated as something that is of God, when, in reality, it's of the devil/ the Antichrist spirit.

So now, do you think it has made its way into the churches?

4

Have You Been Affected?

It's quite obvious at this point that the church will have been affected. But please notice: there were people who were under the influence of the spirit of Antichrist. But there were also people in those churches who were not under this influence. They were still hearing the Spirit and living the way Jesus wanted them to. The big question is: Have you been affected? In most Christians' lives, the correct answer to that is likely yes. Jesus made it plain: we can overcome the influence of the spirit of Antichrist. But it's going to take a close walk with the Holy Spirit and some focused self-discipline to do it. With as deeply as this has been and is continuing to be ingrained into society, to think it has not had any influence or effect upon us is probably wishful thinking. It's trying to pull all of us into its grasp. Sad to say, with way too many, it is succeeding. As I've watched people over the years, there's a progression that I've seen the average Christian move through in their life and this is what it looks like.

The breath of Antichrist works slowly with its ever-present increase and encroachment of wickedness. It is like an ever-increasing pressure that pushes on people to move them away from a Godly scriptural stance and posture in life. It pushes them toward evil and the self-justification of what they are doing.

It works so slowly, and with such deception, the average person has no idea what's happening to them. Over time, we become more and more consumed with our temporal lives, with less and less emphasis being placed on God's purpose and plan for His kingdom on this earth and the spread of the gospel. It becomes something that is no longer about what God is trying to achieve. It has become all about what *we're* trying to achieve (selfishness). If we will take an honest look at ourselves, we have been moved to ways of thinking, motivations, attitudes, and behaviors that we would have never thought we would allow or even embrace into our lives. Let me explain the progression I've seen.

It begins small and then moves toward the ultimate goal:

a. Innocently, it's a slow rearranging of priorities and schedules (for whatever reason) as a nation, community, church, family, and person away from God and what He wants. It continually puts pressure on us to ignore what his Word and his Spirit are telling us that we're to be believing, doing, and living like. It increasingly tries to slide us toward making decisions on the basis of what will benefit us and our family the most.

b. As believers, it encourages making choices without the leading of the Spirit. Using wisdom, of course—just not God's wisdom. We say it's God's wisdom, but unless we have heard from Him, it's actually our wisdom. 1 Corinthians chapter 2 verses 6–16 makes it very clear that as believers, to operate in God's wisdom, we must be hearing or have heard from the Holy Spirit. Anything outside of that is not considered to be God's wisdom.

For unbelievers, God's opinion simply isn't considered. Any scriptural moral basis or directive isn't considered. Decisions are made on a different basis. Again, it will be credited to wisdom and tolerance; but scripturally, it is not.

c. As believers, we may have the thought, "God gave us a mind to think and make choices. We don't have to hear from the Spirit or follow scripture about everything. That makes sense, doesn't it?" To the carnal mind, or the demonically inspired mind, it does make sense. For unbelievers, it may just seem wiser to avoid becoming too religious about life.

d. Our reasoning, intellect, desires, and pride now become big players in our life.

e. Things that are not of God but of the devil's kingdom begin creeping their way into our lives. (Remember, it all begins very innocently.) It doesn't have to be outright sin but simply a reshuffling our focus in life, causing us to spend our time on the things we see as priorities. Very innocently, it begins moving us away from the Holy Spirit's input in our life. We begin making more and more decisions on what we consider to be the best for our life, what makes the most sense. Slowly, we are being groomed into selfishness.

f. As that *iniquity* (bend toward evil in our lives) continues to grow in us, our love and need for God grows less and less (Matthew 24:12).

g. Disobedience to the ways and desires of God begins to steadily increase. Of course, if it grows too much, we'll knock it back because we're Christians. We don't intentionally go out and do something evil. But in truth, we are taking on the perspective of sin management rather than sin elimination. After all, we don't want to get too different from this world. How would we reach them (in reality, we probably haven't gotten anyone saved in years, if ever)? It sounds good to us because it is very self-serving. Since we're under the influence of the spirit of this age (Antichrist), it all makes perfect sense to us.

h. As a result, our relationship with God begins to suffer. Intimacy is leaving. His voice is growing weaker. We aren't increasingly being moved by what moves Him. Our concern for the lost in this world is diminishing. The amount of time we dedicate to eternal fruit grows smaller and smaller.

i. The truth be known, these things will begin growing less and less of a priority in our lives.

> Status quo has entered our life, and we're good with that. It seems like wisdom to us. It makes sense.

j. Now we're on a downhill slide. We're moving quickly toward the bigger goals of the devil. (Remember, he's the one behind this whole thing, including the spirit of Antichrist.)

k. The first big goal: strip Christianity of its power and influence (2 Timothy 3:5). Which really means strip you of your spiritual power and influence. Cause you to become ineffective in your ability to do much of anything to reach the lost. The proof of that is the small amount of Godly spiritual fruit that is following your life. (Very few people being saved. Very few, if any, signs, wonders, or miracles. Very little supernatural.)

l. The next big goal is to cause people to think they don't need Jesus to be ready for eternity. It started with the idea that we don't need the leading of the

Holy Spirit in our lives. In our opinions, we're doing just fine without it. From there, it will move into the thought that we don't need His wisdom. Of course we'd never say that, but He gave us a mind, and we

> Some leaders are actively pursuing to persuade believers that there are more ways to God than just the one, being Jesus. It doesn't make any difference who is saying it; they are under the influence of the spirit of Antichrist.

can think on our own. Also, we don't need Him for everything to remain healthy because we have doctors, therapists, counselors, psychiatrists, etc. We're doing okay financially too. Oh, I'm sure there are areas in which we could do better, but we're okay. And if something goes terribly wrong, we can always turn to the government and get some kind of help from it.

Slowly, slowly, the influence of God and the scripture dissipates. Now we are ripe for the picking. The pace of our demise is quickening. The unrighteous things we are willing to accept into our belief system as righteous, moral, and Godly are beginning to grow quickly. Now we have Christians actually entertaining the thought that there might be more ways to God than just Jesus. Some leaders are actively pursuing to persuade believers that there are more ways to

God than just the one, being Jesus. As we've already discovered, this is the spirit of Antichrist at work. It doesn't make any difference who is saying it; they are under the influence of the spirit of Antichrist.

But since we are being told that true love tolerates pretty much anything in every belief system of this world, we begin to question whether we should be taking such a hard-line stance on Jesus being the only savior for the human race. After all, we don't want to be viewed as intolerant, narrow-minded bigots full of prejudice, or simply unloving people. After all, we need to be open-minded and use some rational intellect as we look at these things. Jesus isn't the only way. After all, who are we to judge?

Thinking that there are other ways to heaven is what makes us fertile ground for deep, deep deception to take over our lives. Now because we were willing to deny the most basic truth, it's difficult to have firm convictions on just about any realm of truth.

m. With the common acceptance of omnitheism and universalism being promoted around the world, if we are not on guard, we will quickly be blinded into thinking these are viable beliefs. Omnitheism is the belief that all religions are basically built around the same God. They may have different names for this God, but in essence, it is the same God.

This philosophy is quickly being accepted in America. The idea being, if we believe in and serve God with different names, that's okay because we're all serving the same God anyway.

Universalism holds that everyone is serving God in their own way, therefore, everyone will be or is already saved. We're being told it's more important to be a good person and member of society than a radical Christian or Jew who thinks their way of salvation is the only way.

n. The last great deception will be when the man known as the Antichrist is promoted as being the embodiment of all gods. He is going to be touted as either the supreme representative of all the deities mankind views as God or, He is God.

o. The biggest goal:

> Eliminate Jesus—as the only Messiah and Savior—from the lives and thinking of the human race. For believers and nonbelievers, it all starts very simply—turn people from being God-centered to being self-centered and selfish.

I have been using the word *selfish* or *selfishness*. To make sure we're on the same page, here are some of my thoughts that sum up what I'm referring to as "selfishness."

- I want my way.
- What I want in life and out of life is the only thing that really matters or matters the most.
- You can think or believe what you want; it won't affect me because I know best. There's really no need to consider your position or beliefs; it's what I think that matters.
- I don't care what you want or prefer; I'm going to do it my way.
- I'm not really interested in what God thinks; my focus is on my own pleasure, happiness, and what entertains me.
- I view life and make decisions on the basis of how it benefits me. This consideration is always first. If it doesn't somehow benefit me; I'm not too interested.

I've seen selfishness defined as "someone who is too concerned with their own welfare or personal interests and having very little concern for another's welfare or interests." It's simply being self-centered.

There is the underlying attitude that the devil is going to use against people in the last days. It's unnerving to watch that attitude of selfishness gain momentum all around us. Isn't it interesting to see the selfishness that Jesus spoke about in Matthew chapter 24 verses 12-13 coming to life around us? It's doing exactly what He said, causing the love for God to grow cold, even pushing it to the point where people who take a stand for God become the focus and must be controlled, silenced, or removed from operating in and having any influence on society. They are viewed as a threat or a menace.

We are watching this happen around us right now. It is gaining in intensity. It is gaining great inroads into influencing and even changing the laws in society. If the spirit of Antichrist is capable of changing laws, it shouldn't surprise us to think that the man—Antichrist—will pursue changing laws (Daniel 7:25).

Here's the shocking part to me: many of the Christian churches in America are accommodating this move toward wickedness. Instead of taking a Godly and scriptural stand against it, we're watching Christianity adapt to this wickedness and welcome it right into the churches. Even though it's clearly ungodly wisdom, we're calling it love and tolerance.

So again I say it: there is the answer to the question we asked earlier, how did we get to this point? We are being influenced and desensitized by an Antichrist spirit and atmosphere that is slowly moving us into a lawless and wicked society. That lawlessness and wickedness is being built on one basic foundation—selfishness. This is exactly what Jesus and Paul said would happen.

We as Christians are not immune to this movement of anti-anointing. That's why we're told over and over don't be deceived. Deception works ever so smoothly and slowly that if we aren't paying attention, it will suck us in. And the worst part is we won't know we've been deceived. It will make so much sense to us. Yet in reality, that wisdom—which is not in line with the scripture—is demonic, no matter how right it may seem (James 3:14–16).

5

Lawlessness

Now we have a clear scriptural basis and understanding that the last days will be a very selfish time.

But *there is a deeper and even more direct connection we need to see.* One of the main characteristics of the man Antichrist will be lawlessness. John alludes to the same characteristic when he's talking about the "spirit of Antichrist." I'm going to go through some verses I touched in the first chapter. A few things I will repeat, but my purpose is to make sure this concept is crystal clear. If we miss this connection, we will not see what Satan's scheme is for our time.

18 "Little children, it is the last time: and as ye have heard that antichrist shall come, even now are there many antichrists; whereby we know that it is the last time. 19 They went out from us, but they were not of us; for if they had been of us, they would no doubt have continued with us: but they went out, that they might be made manifest that they were not all of us" (1 Jn 2:18–19, kjv).

The first thing that John is saying is that when people turn against the anointing, it is because they have succumbed to the power of Antichrist (v. 18: *anti* the *christ*—the anointed one and his anointing). In verse 19, John is saying that the reason some people have left their group was because the power of Antichrist is at work. The fact that they didn't remain with the truth shows they are under the power of Antichrist, and John goes even further to say their leaving makes them Antichrists also (v. 18). That's a big statement!

In chapter 2 verses 20–28, John talks about the true anointing and how it teaches us what truth is and how the anointing will reveal the truth about Jesus being the Messiah. In verse 26, he refers to people trying to lead the believers astray. So the first question the people probably had was this: who are these people under the power of Antichrist, and how will we recognize them? He answers that in verse 29 (niv), "If you know that he is righteous, you know that everyone who does what is right has been born of him."

Now he's introducing a thought that he is going to fully develop in chapter 3. We can recognize whether someone is under the spirit of Antichrist by one simple principle. What is that principle? *Look at what is coming from their lives: righteousness or sin. "Everyone who does what is right has been born of him."*

Watch as John develops on this in chapter 3.

The Breath of Anti-Christ

1 How great is the love the Father has lavished on us, that we should be called children of God! And that is what we are! The reason the world does not know us is that it did not know him. 2 Dear friends, now we are children of God, and what we will be has not yet been made known. But we know that when he appears, we shall be like him, for we shall see him as he is. 3 Everyone who has this hope in him purifies himself, just as he is pure. 4 Everyone who sins breaks the law; in fact, sin is lawlessness. 5 But you know that he appeared so that he might take away our sins. And in him is no sin. 6 No one who lives in him keeps on sinning. No one who continues to sin has either seen him or known him. 7 Dear children, do not let anyone lead you astray. 8 He who does what is right is righteous, just as he is righteous. He who does what is sinful is of the devil, because the devil has been sinning from the beginning. The reason the Son of God appeared was to destroy the devil's work. 9 No one who is born of God will continue to sin, because God's seed remains in him; he cannot go on sinning, because he has been born of God. 10 This is how we know who the children of God are and who the children of the devil are: Anyone who does not do what is right is not a child of God; nor is anyone who does not love his brother. (1 Jn 3:1–10, niv)

Let's look at this verse by verse. I want to make sure you see it clearly.

Verse 1. John states the fact we are called the children of God and know God. It's a result of His love for us. The world (unsaved) doesn't recognize who we really are because they don't know God.

Verse 2. As children of God, when He comes for us, we will be like Him and see Him as He really is.

Verse 3. Everyone who is looking forward to this needs to purify himself. Deal with the sin in their life. He hasn't left the thought he introduced in chapter 2 verse 29. He's simply added the fact that as the children of God, we have a responsibility in this whole process.

Verse 4. When a person breaks the law, they are sinning. In fact *sin is lawlessness.*
This is a key point to where John is going.

Verse 5. Jesus came to take away our sins. He had no sin. So he's saying that Jesus wants nothing to do with sin. He works in the realm of righteousness, not sin.

Verse 6. If we know Jesus and live in Him, we can't keep on sinning. If we do, it shows we don't really know Him and/or haven't seen who He really is. John is beginning to make a clear separation between the characteristics that Jesus will produce in us and the characteristics the Antichrist spirit will produce in us (obedience vs. lawlessness).

Verse 7. Now he's making his point. This is the principle that is to be used to stay out of deception (led astray) in the last days. The principle is in verses 7–10. It is this: *if you do what is right, you are righteous and of God.*

Verse 8. If you sin, you are of the devil. The devil is a sinner, and that's not of Jesus. Jesus came to destroy the devil's work, which is sinning. Remember, sin is lawlessness (v. 4).

Verse 9. The person who is really of God will not *continue* to go on sinning and live in sin. That's not how God operates. It's not of his kingdom. If we are truly born of God, we will reproduce what God is like. God has no sin and does not operate in it.

Verse 10. This is how we know who is under the influence of the spirit of Antichrist. Remember, that's the context of everything John is talking about here. It all centers around whether we do what is right or wrong. If we don't do what is right, we are not children of God, but instead are children of the devil. Also, if we don't love other Christians, we are not of God.

> The spirit of Antichrist is recognized by what the person does. If they continue to live a life of sin (lawlessness), they are under the spirit of Antichrist. If they are purifying themselves (3:3) and endeavoring to do what is right in God's perspective, they are not a person to be considered Antichrist or under its influence.

In the rest of chapter 3, John is talking about love and how it fits into this big picture. He's likely dealing with that because of the people who left the church and those who remained. It's always a painful thing when someone leaves a close-knit group of people. The ones who remained (who are the ones he's writing this letter to) very likely have a lot of questions and need some understanding. So John talks about love and what it acts like. This will help them to hold themselves accountable to what they should do, as well as give some insight as to what happened with the people who left, why they left, and possibly how they left. We will look at this section of scripture again in chapter 8.

In chapter 4 verses 1–6, John is going to very clearly develop on this situation of people leaving the church and what caused them to do it. Let's take a look at it as John explains what took place.

> 1 Dear friends, do not believe every spirit, but test the spirits to see whether they are from God, because many false prophets have gone out into the world. 2 This is how you can recognize the Spirit of God: Every spirit that acknowledges that Jesus Christ has come in the flesh is from God, 3 but every spirit that does not acknowledge Jesus is not from God. This is the spirit of the antichrist, which you have heard is coming and even now is already in the world. 4 You, dear children, are from God and have overcome them, because the one who is in you is greater than the one who is in the world. 5 They are from the world and therefore speak from the viewpoint of the world, and the world listens to them. 6 *We are from God, and whoever knows God*

listens to us; but whoever is not from God does not listen to us. This is how we recognize the Spirit of truth and the spirit of falsehood. (1 Jn 4:1–6, niv)

Verse 1. This is not talking about demonic spirits. There is no indication of that in the context. He's talking about the spirit of Antichrist. When John says we need to test the spirits, he's talking about testing to know if someone is under the influence of the spirit of Antichrist or not. Like we explained earlier in the book, he's talking about testing the human spirit—testing people. Is he referring to the people who left the church (2:18–19)? Looking at the context of this letter, I would say, yes. In chapter 2 verse 19, he uses the same expression: "They went out from us." Are they the same people in his mind? Most likely. But here's the point he is making: the spirits of people need to be tested because many are "false prophets," which means they are under the influence of the wrong spirit. They're under the spirit of Antichrist.

This brings me to two conclusions: (1) there were quite a few who left the church—"many" and (2) they were actively trying to speak into the church and convince the church of their beliefs because he called them "prophets."

Verses 2–3. Here John makes it plain he's talking about the Spirit of God vs. the spirit of Antichrist. If it's the Spirit of God, it will acknowledge that Jesus came in the flesh (context: to be the only Savior of the world). If they do not acknowledge it, they are not of God. They are under the spirit of Antichrist, which he says, by the way, is at work on the earth right now.

So it seems the people who left the church had a problem with Jesus coming to this earth to be the only Savior of it. They didn't accept that, and John is explaining this to the people who remained.

Verse 4. John reassures them they "are of God." They're okay spiritually. This must have been quite a traumatic event that took place in the church. He goes on to say they "have overcome them." *Them* is referring to the ones (false prophets) who left, indicating there was quite a conflict that needed to be overcome. Then he refers back to the spirit realm at work as the reason they "have overcome them." He says the Spirit in you (which would be the Holy Spirit) is greater than the spirit that is in the world (an obvious reference to the Antichrist spirit he's been talking about).

It was the anointing he was talking about in chapter 2 verses 20–27 that caused them to overcome the spirit of Antichrist. We know that the anointing comes from Christ (defined as the Messiah, the Anointed One, and his Anointing). In Luke chapter 4 verse 18 Jesus told us that the anointing came by the Holy Spirit. So the Holy Spirit was obviously at work in the people via the anointing of Jesus, teaching the people from the inside of them that Jesus was the Savior who came to save this world. There is no other savior of the human race.

Verse 5. They (the ones who went out) are of the world, which is under the influence of the Antichrist spirit; therefore, everyone of the world (Antichrist spirit) will listen to their viewpoint. At the end of the verse, John gives the conclusion to the point he has been trying to make: "We are from God, and whoever knows God listens to us; but whoever is not from God does not listen to us. *This is how we recognize the Spirit of truth and the spirit of falsehood*" (1 Jn 4:6, niv).

The spirit of falsehood here is the spirit of Antichrist that he has been talking about. We recognize it by watching how people live their lives:

1. People who are of God listen to them. In the context of these chapters, he is saying they will listen to the message that says they are to purify themselves, live free from sin, do what is right and righteous, acknowledge that Jesus is the only Messiah and way of salvation for the human race, and listen to others who are trying to do the same thing so they'll be ready for Christ's return.

2. People who are of the Antichrist spirit (devil's influence) live in sin and lawlessness (sin is lawlessness—[3:4]). They are not trying to do what is right, they do not acknowledge Jesus being the only way to salvation and heaven. They feel there are other avenues to salvation besides Jesus. And people who are of the Antichrist spirit do not agree with or want to listen to those who proclaim Jesus to be the only way of eternal salvation and are trying to live in love and do what is right.

It is obvious that lawlessness, sin, and the Antichrist spirit are tied together.

But why will lawlessness be acceptable in society? How did society get to the place that they are okay with certain realms of lawlessness? Has it gotten into the church, and are we deceived to the point we are not recognizing it? How does all of that work with a society or church that has become selfish? What is the correlation?

The Holy Spirit asked me a question that opened the whole thing up. He asked: "What sin (or act of lawlessness) is *not* rooted in selfishness?"

With that question, all the lights came on. I could see it. I rattled that question around for weeks in an effort to find a sin or area of lawlessness that was not rooted in selfishness. I couldn't find one. Every example I looked at— if I pushed it deep enough—I found selfishness. Here are some examples:

1. Why does the average person drive faster than the speed limit? (Because they want to.

    Somehow in their mind, it's justified. The bottom line is it's about what they want—selfishness.)

2. Why do people steal? (Because they want to. Somehow in their mind, it's justified. The bottom line is it's about what they want—selfishness.)

3. Why do people lie? (Same answer as above.)

4. Why do people abuse other people? (Same answer as above.)

5. Why do people violate, rape, murder, assault, etc.? (Same answer as above.)

6. Why do Christians gossip, lie, cause strife, get into cliques and dissension, and do a myriad of other things that are no different than the unbeliever? (Same answer as above.)

Here's the shocker:

> Selfishness is where lawlessness draws its power.
>
> Without selfishness, lawlessness is virtually powerless!
>
> Selfishness is the predominant foundation that the spirit of Antichrist is using to build a lawless society.
>
> Selfishness is the spiritual force/wave the Antichrist will ride in to power.

The stage is being set via humanity's selfishness. It has infiltrated every facet of society. It has infiltrated the church. It is operating everywhere, yet we haven't seen it for what it really is: the secret, hidden power of lawlessness. *I'd call that deception.*

Jesus said watch out that you aren't deceived. The problem is we're already operating under a cloud of deception. That's how the Antichrist spirit has gotten into society. It's how it is producing all kinds of lawlessness. The sad part is most people are okay with it, including Christians.

Let me give you a little insight into how it operates. Paul talks about it in 2 Thessalonians. In most of chapter 2, Paul talks about the coming of the man who will be called

> Selfishness is operating everywhere, yet we haven't seen it for what it really is: the secret, hidden power of lawlessness. I'd call that deception.

Antichrist. Paul says he will be the "man of lawlessness" (v. 3). He also calls him the "lawless one"(v. 8). He also addresses what John addressed: the power that is already at work in society (v. 7). The man Antichrist may not be here yet, but the spirit or power of Antichrist is already at work. Paul says:

"Let no one deceive or beguile you in any way, for that day will not come except *the apostasy comes* first [unless *the predicted great falling away* of those who have professed to be Christians has come], and the man of lawlessness (sin) is revealed, who is the son of doom (of perdition)" [Da 7:25, 8:25; 1 Ti 4:1] (2 Thess. 2:3–4, amp; emphasis added).

The niv translates (G646: *apóstasia*) as *rebellion*. This is a bad translation. It should be *falling away* or *apostasy* like it is translated in the *Amplified Version*.

646. ἀποστασία apóstasia, ap-os-tas-ee'-ah; Feminine of the same as 647; *defection from truth* (properly the state), ("apostasy"). :—*falling away, forsake.* (*Strong's Concordance*)

In verses 3–4, Paul is saying that there will be a "great falling away of those who have professed to be Christians." What precipitated that? Why is it going to happen? In verse 7, Paul tells us, "For *the secret power of lawlessness* is already at work" (2 Thess. 2:7, niv; emphasis added).

"Secret power of lawlessness." In context, that's talking about the power to which we have been referring as the "spirit of Antichrist." It is also the thing that caused the great falling away of which Paul spoke in verse 3.

Notice something very important: the main thrust of this is not going to be open rebellion. The main thrust will be done secretly (quietly and hidden).

Look at what the phrase "secret power of lawlessness" really means. Here are the Greek definitions to the words.

The word: "secret":

(G3466) kjv—*mystery*; niv—*secret* (Source: *Strong's Concordance*)

"From a derivative of "muo" *(to shut the mouth); a secret or "mystery"* (through the idea of *silence* imposed by initiation into religious rites)." (emphasis added)

The word: 'lawlessness':

(G458) kjv—*iniquity*; niv—*lawlessness* (Source: *Strong's Concordance*)

"From 459; *illegality*, that is, *violation of law* or (generally) *wickedness*. :—iniquity, X transgress(-ion of) the law, *unrighteousness*." (emphasis added)

(G459) From 1 (as a negative particle) and 3551; *lawless*, that is, (negatively) not subject to (the Jewish) law; (by implication a Gentile), or (positively) wicked. :—*without law, lawless, transgressor, unlawful, wicked*." (emphasis added)

The ("mystery of iniquity"–kjv), "secret power of lawlessness" (niv), or to use another meaning in the definition, the "silent" power of lawlessness is exactly what? Here is a little picture of how this "secret power" will operate.

a. This wickedness is not going to operate as open, willful rebellion. It won't be loud, noisy, and demanding to be heard.

b. This is going to be operating quietly below the surface. It won't be talked about for what it really is—lawlessness. Yet it is being and will be promoted. It has taken the faces of tolerance, universalism, and omnitheism . The actual working of this lawlessness will be secret or quiet.

c. Here is how it operates: wickedness or lawlessness slowly erodes away at our all-out 100 percent submission to God. It undermines it and tries to stop it. That's why there will be a "great falling away" of Christians from the Lord Jesus Christ (verses 1 and 3). Without that submission to God (which has been replaced by lawlessness), we become deceived, and our love for God grows cold. We leave our first love, which is pursuing what pleases God with all our heart, soul, mind, and strength, and begin to live our lives according to what pleases us (selfishness). Jesus talked about this in Matthew 24.

d. *The secret power of lawlessness if selfishness!*

And this is what it produces in mankind:

And *because iniquity shall abound, the love of many shall wax cold*. But he that shall endure unto the end, the same shall be saved. (Mt 24:12–13, kjv; emphasis added)

Because of the increase of wickedness, the love of most will grow cold, but he who stands firm to the end will be saved. (Mt 24:12–13, niv; emphasis added)

And *the love of the great body of people will grow cold because of the multiplied lawlessness and iniquity.* But he who endures to the end will be saved. (Mt 24:12–13, amp; emphasis added)

Selfishness is a force that can operate very quietly. As it works in people, it can cause them to get out front and publicly lead and make large public displays. But for the most part, when the average person operates under the power of selfishness, they are not trying to draw a lot of attention to themselves. The reason: because most of the time, it has to do with breaking the law or disregarding the expectations of someone in authority, or someone with whom we have a commitment/partnership.

The conclusion I want you to see is that as long as the laws of the land stand for righteousness, the selfish areas of sin try to operate quietly, silently, and undiscovered. Selfishness tries to get what it wants or its own way in a quiet manner. That is still what is primarily happening in America now. Even though the righteous laws of the land are being attacked and eroded, there is still a system of law

> The changing of righteous laws into a system of laws that basically supports lawlessness (from God's perspective in Scripture) should stand out as one of the most obvious indications we are under the influence of the Antichrist spirit.

that reflects righteousness. In that type of setting, to do your own thing (selfishness) and break those laws requires a person to do it in secret as much as possible. Otherwise you get caught and will pay the consequences. We are watching this scenario take place around us everyday. People secretly trying to get away with breaking the law. It's a reality that stares each one of us in the face on a daily basis. It supports the fact that the secret power of lawlessness is selfishness, and it tries to operate in relative secrecy!

With that principle in mind it should come as no surprise why people are trying to change the laws of the land, replacing Godly laws with ungodly ones. That way what is being done will no longer be considered lawlessness, and they won't have to hide it. The deeper we get into the last days, the attack on Godly laws will grow more vicious. The changing of righteous laws into a system of laws that basically supports lawlessness (from God's perspective in scripture) should stand out as one of the most obvious indications we are under the influence of the Antichrist spirit. It was this influence of the spirit of Antichrist that solidly expressed itself in America creating the strong separation of church and state, removal of prayer from schools, etc. Why would I say that? Allow me to explain: it was the influence of Godliness and righteous laws that kept this country on track spiritually. To reconstruct the legal system by creating laws that are contrary to God's standard, you must first remove his influence from society. If that isn't done, the general public won't allow the switch to take place. The removal of the Godly influence has been and still is taking place in America, and it's all happening under the guise of tolerance, non-discrimination, equal rights, etc. The more the influence of the Christian God can be removed from society, the easier it is to create a system of government and laws that are contrary to Biblical standards. What is the result of that? A society that no longer has to hide its sin. They don't have to keep it a secret.

It can be brought out into the open and publicly displayed. That's what we are seeing take place in America right now.

That reconstruction of law is foundational to the wave of rebellion and lawlessness which Paul spoke about in 2 Thessalonians chapter 2. It will create the power base needed for the man "Antichrist" to come into power. The restructuring of law and governments to support what Jehovah God considers lawless behavior will continue to increase. It will produce a worldwide society that is rebellious against God.

It's how the spirit of Antichrist or lawlessness operates. When the man Antichrist comes, he will do the same thing—change the laws. In Daniel 7:25, there is a prophecy concerning the Antichrist, and it says he will try to change the set times and the laws. The Bible says the Antichrist spirit is very lawless and will produce a man who is also very lawless. It is currently happening all around us. The sad part is most people (including Christians) don't recognize what is happening to us. Yet the whole while, we are being slowly herded toward the one-world system, which the Antichrist will use as his platform.

> Lawlessness receives its power from selfishness!
> Selfishness is operating under the power of Antichrist.
> Selfishness is one of the greatest tools of deception in the last days.

Like any other form of deception, it's very difficult to see where we are deceived *because we* are *deceived.*

A huge problem with selfishness that encourages deception is this: selfishness isn't looking for what's right or truth. In many cases, it already knows. Selfishness tries to conceal and hide what it's doing. Selfishness tries to find ways to secretly get away with doing what is wrong. It operates under a smokescreen of deception. That's why it's so easy for selfish people to be deceived. They are willfully living in deception already. By their own choices, they are trying to deceive others and keep them from seeing what's really going on in their lives. So it's very easy for the Antichrist deception to come upon them. The landing pad of deception has already been built and is being well maintained in their life. Adding more and more deception to that type of person is very easy.

The lawlessness that is infiltrating the world, every nation, every community, and trying to get into every person is a plant that is growing out of the roots of selfishness.

That's why it's so easy for selfish people to be deceived. They are willfully living in deception already.

No wonder there are so many scriptures that are written to expose what the End Times are going to be like that concentrate on one huge characteristic—selfishness. It's at the root of the whole thing!

6

Wisdom

While the Lord was showing these things to me, I was reading one day, and these scriptures took on a whole new meaning.

> 13 Who is wise and understanding among you? Let him show it by his good life, by deeds done in the humility that comes from wisdom. 14 But if you harbor *bitter envy* and *selfish ambition* in your hearts, do not boast about it or deny the truth. 15 Such "wisdom" does not come down from heaven but is earthly, unspiritual, of the devil. 16 For where you have *envy* and *selfish ambition*, there you find disorder and every evil practice. (James 3:13–16, niv; emphasis added)

You probably have noticed it already. As James is talking about wisdom, he brings up the topic of selfishness. His point is that the wrong kind of wisdom will produce bitter envy and selfish ambition. Then he makes a statement in verse 15 that probably every Christian believes: envy and selfish ambition are of the devil. So I went back to the Old Testament and read a couple of accounts that describe the characteristics of Lucifer before his fall. Let's take a look at these scriptures, and then I want to point out something that is very interesting.

> How you have fallen from heaven, O morning star, son of the dawn! You have been cast down to the earth, you who once laid low the nations! You said in your heart, "*I will* ascend to heaven; *I will* raise my throne above the stars of God; *I will* sit enthroned on the mount of assembly, on the utmost heights of the sacred mountain. *I will* ascend above the tops of the clouds; *I will* make myself like the Most High." But you are brought down to the grave, to the depths of the pit. (Isa. 14:12–15, niv; emphasis added)

Here we see what was motivating Lucifer. Notice how many times he said "I will." Who is he concerned about? Was he wanting what God wanted, or what he wanted? We know the answer is he was disregarding what God wanted and exerting his own will. So what is that? It's selfishness.

Next is a section of scripture that is attributed to the king of Tyre. Yet what Ezekiel describes cannot apply to a human being. Most scholars feel its direct application is to Lucifer, which would make sense when you take a close look at the description. That's the perspective from which we're going to view it.

> The word of the Lord came to me: "Son of man, take up a lament concerning the king of Tyre and say to him: 'This is what the Sovereign Lord says: "You were the model of perfection, *full of wisdom* and perfect in beauty. You were in Eden, the garden of God; every precious stone adorned you: ruby, topaz and emerald, chrysolite, onyx and jasper, sapphire, turquoise and beryl. Your settings and mountings were made of gold; on the day you were created they were prepared. You were anointed as a guardian cherub, for so I ordained you. You were on the holy mount of God; you walked among the fiery stones. You were blameless in your ways from the day you were created till wickedness was found in you. Through your widespread trade you were filled with violence, and you sinned. So I drove you in disgrace from the mount of God, and I expelled you, O guardian cherub, from among the fiery stones. *Your heart became proud on account of your beauty, and you corrupted your wisdom because of your splendor.* So I threw you to the earth; I made a spectacle of you before kings." (Ezekiel 28:11–17, niv; emphasis added)

Notice, God references Lucifer as being full of wisdom. The thing that corrupted his wisdom was his pride. His amazing perfection, beauty, and splendor blinded his true wisdom and caused him to begin thinking selfishly. Because of his splendor, Lucifer actually believed he deserved to be equal with God. As a result, he took on the characteristics that James described: "bitter envy and selfish ambition." These became the motivating forces in his life. Bitter describes the type of envy that developed in him. *Envy* can be defined as "being discontent with what you have and being resentful or having negative feelings toward someone because of what they have."

Lucifer became envious of God. He wanted what God had. He was thinking about himself. Envy is typically driven by selfishness. What you have, I want. It's about me. Selfishness.

Lucifer's envy caused him to be motivated by selfish ambition. Basically, he went after something that didn't belong to him. It belonged to God, but he wanted it for himself. So again, what are we looking at? Selfishness. That's why James called it selfish ambition.

The core of this selfishness that the human race is dealing with actually originated with Lucifer. The Antichrist spirit is also of the devil. The entire plan of the Antichrist spirit in the last days has been brewed up by Satan. Since the whole thing is anti (against) Christ (the Messiah), it becomes really clear what is going on. This Antichrist spirit is nothing more than a form of the "bitter envy and selfish ambition," which caused Satan to be thrown out of heaven in the first place. It's simply recycling with a different face.

The result is a corrupt form of wisdom. It's ungodly. It's unrighteous. It's rooted in envy and ambitions that are selfish. The problem is the earth is full of it, including the church. Allow me to show that to you. Let's begin by looking at that whole section of scripture in James.

> 13 Who is wise and understanding among you? Let him show it by his good life, by *deeds done in the humility that comes from wisdom*. 14 But if you harbor *bitter envy* and *selfish ambition* in your hearts, do not boast about it or deny the truth. 15 *Such "wisdom" does not come down from heaven but is earthly, unspiritual, of the devil.* 16 For where you have envy and selfish ambition, there you find disorder and every evil practice. 17 *But the wisdom that comes from heaven* is first of all pure; then peace-loving, considerate, submissive, full of mercy and good fruit, impartial and sincere. 18 Peacemakers who sow in peace raise a harvest of righteousness. (Jas 3:13–18, niv; emphasis added)

James is pointing out there are two kinds of wisdom. One wisdom comes from God. The other wisdom comes from the devil. God's wisdom produces a harvest of righteousness. The devil's wisdom produces disorder and every evil practice. When you lay the definition of lawlessness against these two kinds of wisdom, it is easy to see which kind of wisdom created and formed lawlessness. Depending upon which kind of wisdom we use, we will either begin to think like God, or we will take on the spirit of Antichrist and begin thinking like the devil, who at his core is selfish.

I don't know of too many people whose goal is to be a fool. Most everybody wants to be wise in how they think, what they do, and how they live. But true wisdom comes only from God. The question is "how do we get it?" I know that James 1:5 says we are to ask God, and He will give it to us. But my question goes beyond that into "what is 'true wisdom' like?" I want to know under which wisdom I'm operating. The areas in which I'm under the wrong wisdom need to be changed. Let's look at a few scriptures that will help us with that.

> 5 For *those who are according to the flesh and are controlled by its unholy desires set their minds on and pursue those things which gratify the flesh*, but *those who are according to the Spirit and are controlled by the desires of the Spirit set their minds on and seek those things which gratify the [Holy] Spirit*. 6 Now *the mind of the flesh [which is sense and reason without the Holy Spirit]* is death [death that comprises all the miseries arising from sin, both here and hereafter]. But *the mind of the [Holy] Spirit is life and [soul] peace* [both now and forever]. 7 [That is] because *the mind of the flesh* [with its carnal thoughts and purposes] is hostile to God, for it *does not submit itself to God's Law; indeed it cannot*. (Rom 8:5–7, amp; emphasis added)

This section of scripture has a lot of information in it. I don't want to touch it piece by piece, but there are a few things that will help us in seeing under which wisdom we are operating: the pure wisdom that is from God, or the corrupted wisdom that is of the devil/the flesh.

Here again we have the two sides being shown. Paul is talking about the same two kinds of wisdom that James was talking about. The only difference is that Paul is showing that it works through our minds. We choose to which wisdom we are going to submit. If we go with the desires and cravings of the flesh/old nature, it will bring death into our lives. If we go with the Holy Spirit and what He wants, it will bring life and soul peace.

Right in the middle of these verses, Paul makes a statement that is huge! He says the wrong kind of thinking (wisdom) is *"sense and reason without the Holy Spirit."* Since God's wisdom can only come via the Holy Spirit, any wisdom that is not by the Holy Spirit comes from a different spirit. That's what James was referring to. It's either Godly wisdom or its origin is the devil. There is no middle ground.

When we're reasoning our way through things (it makes sense and seems reasonable to us), but we haven't received any direction from the Holy Spirit (yet somehow it makes sense to us), we're actually under demonic influence. That's how the spirit of Antichrist works on us and influences us. It's an ever-present input that says, "This seems like the wise thing to do." It makes sense to us. In reality, we are not forming our conclusion on anything that has to do with the input of the Holy Spirit. In fact, we may be forming our conclusion on something that is completely contrary to the Holy Spirit. Paul explains this a little more deeply in the next scripture.

> *6 We do, however, speak a message of wisdom among the mature, but not the wisdom of this age or of the rulers of this age, who are coming to nothing. 7 No, we speak of God's secret wisdom, a wisdom that has been hidden and that God destined for our glory before time began. 8 None of the rulers of this age understood it, for if they had, they would not have crucified the Lord of glory. 9 However, as it is written: "No eye has seen, no ear has heard, no mind has conceived what God has prepared for those who love him"— 10 but God has revealed it to us by his Spirit. The Spirit searches all things, even the deep things of God. 11 For who among men knows the thoughts of a man except the man's spirit within him? In the same way no one knows the thoughts of God except the Spirit of God. 12 We have not received the spirit of the world but the Spirit who is from God, that we may understand what God has freely given us. 13 This is what we speak, not in words taught us by human wisdom but in words taught by the Spirit, expressing spiritual truths in spiritual words. 14 The man without the Spirit does not accept the things that come from the Spirit of God, for they are foolishness to him, and he cannot understand them, because they are spiritually discerned. 15 The spiritual man makes judgments about*

all things, but he himself is not subject to any man's judgment: 16 "For who has known the mind of the Lord that he may instruct him?" But we have the mind of Christ. (1 Cor. 2:6–16, niv; *emphasis added)*

Again, there is a tremendous amount of information in that passage of scripture. I don't want to look at everything in that passage, but I do want to point out a few things.

First of all, notice the two types of wisdom. One comes from God (v. 7); the other is the wisdom from this age and the rulers of this age (v. 6).

Secondly, God reveals His wisdom to us by the Holy Spirit (v. 10, 11, 13, 14).

Thirdly, the wisdom of this age and the rulers of this age are also referred to as human wisdom in verse 13. The person who operates under this kind of wisdom does not understand the things that come from God. They are foolishness to him because the only way they can be understood is by the Holy Spirit.

Please notice this: human wisdom is equated with the wisdom of this age and the rulers of this age. Why? Because that's where it comes from (cf. James 3:13–16).

Here's the point we must remember:

No matter how much something may make sense to us, if we have not received God's input on the situation by the Holy Spirit, we're probably in human wisdom (1 Cor. 2:13), which is sense and reasoning without the Holy Spirit ("mind of the flesh" [Romans 8:6]), which is earthly, unspiritual, and of the devil (James 3:15).

This is what is happening around us on a daily basis. Society and the church are moving further and further away from the Holy Spirit and the foundation of the scripture into the spirit of Antichrist. Only about 25 percent of American Christians strongly believe in the existence of the Holy Spirit as a living entity, while an additional 9 percent somewhat believe in the existence of the Holy Spirit as a living entity. (source: Barna Group, April 13, 2009, article: "Most American Christians do not Believe that Satan or the Holy Spirit Exist") That is only one out of every four Christians who are convinced the Holy Spirit is alive and not just a force of some kind.

This is a direct result of the spirit of Antichrist that has been at work among us. If the Antichrist spirit is *anti* the *anointing*, it would make sense that this spirit is trying to move us away from the Holy Spirit. The anointing comes via the Holy Spirit (Luke 4:18, 1 John 2:20–27). For the Antichrist spirit to increase among us, the emphasis on the Holy Spirit must decrease. This will continue to get worse as we move further into the last days.

The push is to make our selfishness sound reasonable to us. It makes sense to us. It's wisdom. With it comes an increase in lawlessness, and the end result is what Jesus spoke about:

> 9 Then they will hand you over to suffer affliction and tribulation and put you to death, and you will be hated by all nations for My name's sake. 10 And then many will be offended and repelled and will begin to distrust and desert [Him Whom they ought to trust and obey] and will stumble and fall away and betray one another and pursue one another with hatred. 11 And many false prophets will rise up and deceive and lead many into error. 12 And *the love of the great body of people will grow cold because of the multiplied lawlessness and iniquity*, 13 But he who endures to the end will be saved. (Mt 24:9–13, amp; emphasis added)

Verse 9 is happening in the world right now. Christians are being openly martyred.

We are at the beginning of verse 10. Offense and being repelled for taking a solid biblical stand for Jesus is well under way around the world, and it is beginning to take place in America.

Verse 11 is happening right now. We have so-called Christian leaders saying that Islam (besides the other religions that are being promoted as capable of producing eternal life) is also a valid belief system that will get mankind to heaven.

Verse 12 is the main verse I want to address in this passage. It says that lawlessness turns the love (agape, love for God) of the people cold. Did you catch that? Jesus specifically named "lawlessness," which we now know comes from selfishness. He said lawlessness will turn the hearts of the believers "cold" in their love for God. We are watching this happen around us in alarming numbers, especially in the younger generations. They are leaving the church in record numbers (source: Barna Research Group, *You Lost Me*). Did they know God and turn on Him? That would seem the viable conclusion according to what Jesus said was going to happen.

So now I need to ask why would that happen? How can someone know God and then turn away from Him and simply follow the bend in their old nature (iniquity) away from God and into sin? I believe a large part of the answer to that is found in a scripture to which we already referred. Let me refer to it again, and this time I want to emphasize something different than I did before.

> 6 *We do, however, speak a message of wisdom among the mature, but not the wisdom of this age or of the rulers of this age, who are coming to nothing.* 7 *No, we speak of God's secret wisdom, a wisdom that has been hidden and that God destined for our glory before time began.* 8 *None of the rulers of this age understood it, for if they had, they would not have crucified the Lord of glory.* 9 *However, as it is written: "No eye has seen, no ear has heard, no mind has conceived what God has prepared for those who love him"*—10 *but God has revealed it to us by his Spirit. The Spirit searches all things, even the deep things of God.* 11 *For who among men knows the thoughts of a man except the man's spirit within*

him? In the same way no one knows the thoughts of God except the Spirit of God. 12 We have not received the spirit of the world but the Spirit who is from God, that we may understand what God has freely given us. 13 This is what we speak, not in words taught us by human wisdom but in words taught by the Spirit, expressing spiritual truths in spiritual words. 14 The man without the Spirit does not accept the things that come from the Spirit of God, for they are foolishness to him, and he cannot understand them, because they are spiritually discerned. 15 The spiritual man makes judgments about all things, but he himself is not subject to any man's judgment: 16 "For who has known the mind of the Lord that he may instruct him?" But we have the mind of Christ. (1 Cor 2:6–16, niv; *emphasis added)*

They knew the programs that were in the church. They attended youth group. They helped feed the homeless. They were at church on a consistent basis. But did they know the Holy Spirit? Were they living in revelations of the Spirit? Did they ever get to know the Holy Spirit on an experiential level, or was it all head-knowledge? Did they really understand spiritual things and Godly wisdom, or did it seem foolish to them? They never really got it. The problem that has developed is that we are no longer emphasizing the Holy Spirit and His purpose the way we should. There are probably many reasons for this, but the *real reason* it is taking place in the churches in America is because we've fallen under the influence or pressure of the Antichrist spirit. Not emphasizing the Holy Spirit just seems to make sense to us. It's too controversial. It's not seeker friendly. I mean, stop and think about it: God wouldn't want us to do something that would scare people away from church. And it seems the Holy Spirit sometimes does that. It just seems like it's wisdom and reasonable.

We've been deceived! If there's one person who wants people to know the Father—and will work to that end with everything within him—it's the Holy Spirit. It's the reason He was sent. But yet in our earthly wisdom, we feel we need to protect people from the Holy Spirit. I say it again, we've been deceived!

7

This is How We Know!

Jesus was very concerned about people being deceived in the last days. He stated it numerous times.

> Jesus answered: *"Watch out that no one deceives you.* For many will come in my name, claiming, "I am the Christ," *and will deceive many.* (Mt 24:4–5, niv; emphasis added)
>
> At that time many will turn away from the faith and will betray and hate each other, and many false prophets will appear *and deceive many people.* (Mt 24:10–11, niv; emphasis added)
>
> If those days had not been cut short, no one would survive, but for the sake of the elect those days will be shortened. At that time if anyone says to you, "Look, here is the Christ!" or, "There he is!" do not believe it. For false Christs and false prophets will appear and perform great signs and miracles *to deceive even the elect*—if that were possible. See,

> I have told you ahead of time. (Mt 24:22–25, niv; emphasis added)
>
> Jesus said to them: "*Watch out that no one deceives you. Many will come in my name, claiming, 'I am he,' and will deceive many.*" (Mk 13:5–6, niv; emphasis added)
>
> He replied: "*Watch out that you are not deceived.* For many will come in my name, claiming, 'I am he,' and, 'The time is near.' Do not follow them." (Lk 21:8, niv; emphasis added)

The Apostle Paul was concerned about it.

> Not to become easily unsettled or alarmed by some prophecy, report or letter supposed to have come from us, saying that the day of the Lord has already come. *Don't let anyone deceive you* in any way, for [that day will not come] until the rebellion occurs and the man of lawlessness is revealed, the man doomed to destruction. (2 Thes 2:2–3, niv; emphasis added)
>
> The coming of the lawless one will be in accordance with the work of Satan displayed in all kinds of counterfeit miracles, signs and wonders, and *in every sort of evil that deceives* those who are perishing. They perish because they refused to love the truth and so be saved. (2 Thess 2:9–10, niv; emphasis added)
>
> The Spirit clearly says that in later times some will abandon the faith and follow *deceiving spirits* and things taught by demons. (1 Tim 4:1, niv; emphasis added)

The Breath of Anti-Christ

John was concerned about deception and the Antichrist.

> *Many deceivers, who do not acknowledge Jesus Christ as coming in the flesh, have gone out into the world. Any such person is the deceiver and the antichrist.* (2 Jn 1:7, niv; emphasis added)

> Because of the signs he was given power to do on behalf of the first beast, *he deceived the inhabitants of the earth.* He ordered them to set up an image in honor of the beast who was wounded by the sword and yet lived. (Rev. 13:14, niv; emphasis added)

What should we do to ensure we are not deceived? Are there any guidelines that would help us?

Over the course of the previous chapters, we have given you a number of ways to recognize deception as well as guard yourself against it. But let me reemphasize a few more things that will help ensure we are not deceived.

John had the same concern. He voiced it in 2 John 7 (see above). Since he and Paul had the most to say about the Antichrist/man of lawlessness, let's look at what they had to say about protecting ourselves from the deceit that will be happening in connection with the power of Antichrist or the man Antichrist himself.

John addresses the spirit or power of Antichrist. He says it has been on the earth since he was on this earth. It has been gaining momentum, and it is obviously a strong influence in the world today. The Holy Spirit gave some very pointed advice and input (via John) concerning how believers should view what's happening around them in the last days so they won't be deceived. Let's take a look at it. I call these the 'this-is-how-we-know' scriptures.

"*We know* that we have come to know him if we obey his commands. The man who says, 'I know him,' but does not do what he commands is a liar, and the truth is not in him. But if anyone obeys his word, God's love is truly made complete in him. *This is how we know* we are in him: Whoever claims to live in him must walk as Jesus did" (1 Jn 2:3–6, niv; emphasis added).

How will we know if someone is really a believer and knows the Lord or not? Do they obey? Are they obeying the scriptural directives for believers? If someone knows Jesus, it is marked by obedience in their lives. We can tell who is being truthful and who is lying to us via this principle. The thing we are looking for is how they live out their Christian life:

18 "Dear children, this is the last hour; and as you have heard that the antichrist is coming, even now many antichrists have come. *This is how we know* it is the last hour. 19 They went out from us, but they did not really belong to us. For if they had belonged to us, they would have remained with us; but their going showed that none of them belonged to us" (1 Jn 2:18–19, niv; emphasis added).

Verse 18. Even back in John's time, the process was underway. He was also part of the last times, and this was proven by the many people who are *anti* the *Christ*. They had fallen under the pervasive power of this time. In this section of scripture, John is talking about people who have become Antichrist, or literally *anti* the Christ (the Messiah/anointing). This indicator is quite simple: anyone who is against Jesus being the only Messiah—and/or they don't believe in the anointing—is of the Antichrist spirit.

Verse 19. A division was and still is taking place because of the people who have been influenced by the Antichrist spirit. John describes them as either belonging to the church or not belonging. If they have left, it was an indication that they didn't really belong to or were a part of the church. *Belong* is an important word. It comes from two Greek words (*Strong's*: G1510 and G2258), which indicate "I exist in agreement." The indicator of being under Antichrist power is leaving a church over issues concerning Jesus being the only Savior of the world, or not believing in or accepting the anointing of Jesus.

"*If you know* that He is righteous, *you know* that everyone who does what is right has been born of Him" (1 Jn 2:29, niv; emphasis added). If we are a believer, we know that Jesus is righteous. The Holy Spirit and the Word have made that plain to us. As a result of that, if we are looking for the people who have been truly born of Christ (born again), we look for those who have taken on His nature and are doing what is right.

"Dear friends, now we are children of God, and what we will be has not yet been made known. But *we know* that when He appears, we shall be like Him, for we shall see Him as He is. Everyone who has this hope in him purifies himself, just as He is pure" (1 Jn 3:2–3, niv; emphasis added). Even though we are God's children, we still don't know what we will be like when He comes. We do know this: when He appears, we will be like Him, and we will see Him just as He is. The true children of God have this realization and hope, and therefore, they purify themselves to be ready for Jesus when He returns. If you want to know if someone is really a child of God, look for the person who is continually at work on their obedience and purity.

"*This is how we know* who the children of God are and who the children of the devil are: Anyone who does not do what is right is not a child of God; nor is anyone who does not love his brother" (1 Jn 3:10, niv; emphasis added).

Evidently, sin will be an increasingly huge problem the closer we get to the return of Jesus. In verses 4–9, John is addressing this issue quite directly. In verse 4, he says everyone who breaks the law has sinned. In fact, he says, "Sin is lawlessness." In verse 7, he says, "Do not let anyone lead you astray." Then he goes on to say that if people are doing what is right, it is an indication that they are righteous. Those who persist in being involved in sin are of the devil (his kingdom). In verse 9, he says that a person truly born of God cannot continue/persist in their sin. Then in verse 10, he makes a very bold and blunt statement. He tells us exactly how to tell if someone is a genuine believer or not. It all ties back into obedience, doing what is right, and loving other believers.

"*We know* that we have passed from death to life, because we love our brothers. Anyone who does not love remains in death. Anyone who hates his brother is a murderer, and you know that no murderer has eternal life in him" (1 Jn 3:14–15, niv; emphasis added). One of the things to watch for is this: how are Christians getting along? True believers will make an effort to love each other and treat each other accordingly. Any believers who actually hate other believers (or in my opinion, hate anyone) are not genuine believers. Scripture teaches us to have compassion for others, not hate.

"*This is how we know* what love is: Jesus Christ laid down his life for us. And we ought to lay down our lives for our brothers" (1 Jn 3:16, niv; emphasis added). This is still in the context of loving one another. True love will lay down its own *life* (Gr.–psuche–*Strong's* 5590). This word is defined as "breath, soul, the seat of the feelings, desires, affections, aversions;" it's desires, feelings, etc. for the other person. As Jesus did it for us, we are to be doing it for others. Then in verse 17–18, he gives an example: "If anyone has material possessions and sees his brother in need but has no pity on him, how can the love of God be in him? Dear children, let us not love with words or tongue but with actions and in truth" (1 Jn 3:17–18, niv).

He's saying that if we truly love someone, we will do something to help that person if they are in need. Talk is cheap. Anyone can say *I love you*. But we know it's the truth when it produces actions. Then John says that taking action on someone's behalf is the measure of whether we are really in the truth or not. See the next verse.

"*This then is how we know* that we belong to the truth" (1 Jn 3:19, niv; emphasis added).

John was not only concerned about the people recognizing who the other true believers were; he knew they would also want to be sure that they are okay spiritually to make sure they haven't been deceived. The following verses address that concern, and John is explaining how they can take inventory of their own lives to be sure they are personally doing well.

"And this is His command: to believe in the name of his Son, Jesus Christ, and to love one another as He commanded us. Those who obey His commands live in Him, and He in them. And *this is how we know* that He lives in us: *We know it* by the Spirit He gave us" (1 Jn 3:23–24, niv; emphasis added).

The command is in verse 23. If we obey His commands, we live in Him and He in us (v. 24). We know He lives in us by the Holy Spirit He gave to us because it's by the Holy Spirit that He lives in us, and we live in Him. So another way of knowing if someone is of God or of the Antichrist is by the spirit that lives in him. The Holy Spirit lives in believers, and He helps us obey. The Antichrist spirit lives in unbelievers, and they do not obey God or do what is right in His sight.

The Breath of Anti-Christ

"*This is how you can recognize* the Spirit of God: Every spirit that acknowledges that Jesus Christ has come in the flesh is from God, but every spirit that does not acknowledge Jesus is not from God. This is the spirit of the antichrist, which you have heard is coming and even now is already in the world" (1 Jn 4:2–3, niv; emphasis added). Take this verse in context of what John said in chapter 2. He was talking about the source of our salvation—the Messiah. Here he says the Spirit of God will say that Jesus came in the flesh. Remember to connect that statement with chapter 2 and why He came to this world in the flesh. He came as our Messiah and Savior. Tie this back into the gospel of John chapter 1, where it is talking about Jesus having come in the flesh. What does it say there as to why He came? To be the light and life of our salvation. He came to bring salvation (Messiah). The Spirit of God will acknowledge this, and anyone under the Spirit's influence will agree. The person under the spirit of Antichrist will not acknowledge this. This is how you can tell who is who.

"We are from God, and whoever knows God listens to us; but whoever is not from God does not listen to us. *This is how we recognize* the Spirit of truth and the spirit of falsehood" (1 Jn 4:6, niv; emphasis added). When it comes to this issue of through whom salvation comes (which has been the main focus of ch. 2 v. 18 – ch. 4 v. 6), John says the people who know God, His anointing (ch. 2 vv. 21, 26, 27), and His Spirit (ch. 3 v. 24, ch. 4 v. 2) will listen to the ones who are proclaiming Jesus is the *only* way to heaven and that He is the *only* Messiah. This is how we recognize the Spirit of truth. These people are not deceived under the counterfeit anointing (ch. 2 v. 27). They are not under the delusion and influence of the spirit of Antichrist: "This is how we recognize the spirit of truth and the spirit of falsehood." (In context, spirit of falsehood is referring to the spirit of Antichrist.)

The people who don't listen to this message of Jesus being the only Way to the Father or do not agree with it are not of God. They are of the counterfeit anointing (ch. 2 v. 27); they are of the spirit of falsehood. They are of the Antichrist spirit (ch. 4 v. 3). They are the ones to whom John was referring in chapter 2 verse 19—the ones who left them (the church). *This is the main way we recognize and test the spirit of Antichrist. The people who are under the Antichrist spirit say that Jesus is not the only Messiah or the only way of salvation. This is how you recognize truth from falsehood.*

"*We know* that we live in Him and He in us, because He has given us of His Spirit. And we have seen and testify that the Father has sent His Son to be the Savior of the world. If anyone acknowledges that Jesus is the Son of God, God lives in him and he in God. *And so we know* and rely on the love God has for us. God is love. Whoever lives in love lives in God, and God in him" (1 Jn 4:13–16, niv; emphasis added). One of the assurances we have that we are still okay with God and that we are not deceived is having the Holy

Spirit living in us. With that knowledge, we know and can rely on God's love for us. God will see us through.

"Everyone who believes that Jesus is the Christ is born of God, and everyone who loves the father loves His child as well. *This is how we know* that we love the children of God: by loving God and carrying out His commands. This is love for God: to obey His commands. And His commands

> This is the main way we recognize and test the spirit of Antichrist. The people who are under the Antichrist spirit say that Jesus is not the only Messiah or the only way of salvation. This is how you recognize truth from falsehood.

are not burdensome. (1 Jn 5:1–3, niv; emphasis added)" John is still dealing with the characteristics of a person who is doing well spiritually. He is giving principles against which we are to measure ourselves so that we can know we are loving each other. We know we are loving each other if we are loving God and carrying out His commands. Love for God is to obey His commands.

"I write these things to you who believe in the name of the Son of God so *that you may know* that you have eternal life" (1 Jn 5:13, niv; emphasis added). John is simply stating the reason for the last portion of this book. He wants them to be secure in their own salvation and set their hearts at ease.

In the book of 1 John, he is addressing two major themes:

1. How we can recognize if people are under the Spirit of God or the spirit of Antichrist. This is important in the last days so no one is led astray or deceived. John gives characteristics by which we can make that determination.
2. How we can recognize if we are still doing well spiritually, or whether we have become ensnared by the spirit of Antichrist. It's not of God that we live in fear, but as we are perfected in His love, it will drive out any fear so our hearts can be at ease. So again, John gives characteristics against which we can measure ourselves to make that determination.

His thoughts even spill over into the second book. Here John says,

> And now, dear lady, I am not writing you a new command but one we have had from the beginning. I ask that we love one another. And this is love: that we walk in obedience to His commands. As you have heard from the beginning, His command is that you walk in love. *Many deceivers, who do not acknowledge Jesus Christ as coming in the flesh, have gone out into the world. Any such person is the deceiver and the antichrist.* Watch out that you do not lose what you have worked for, but that you may be rewarded fully.

> Anyone who runs ahead and does not continue in the teaching of Christ does not have God; whoever continues in the teaching has both the Father and the Son. (2 Jn 5–9, niv; emphasis added)

It's obvious this topic is still on his mind. He doesn't want anyone deceived by what's happening in the last days, so he again gives some principles on how to be wise and be on guard.

We are living in the days he was talking about. *How do we know* whether it's God's Spirit or the spirit of Antichrist at work among us? These principles were written for our time. We'd do well to know and memorize them because this is how we know.

8

Paul's Concern

The Apostle Paul gives numerous insights and warnings concerning the time in which we live and what lies ahead. We'll look at a few of these scriptures and see what Paul had to say.

> 1 Now, brothers, about times and dates we do not need to write to you, 2 for you know very well that the day of the Lord will come like a thief in the night. 3 *While people are saying, "Peace and safety," destruction will come on them suddenly, as labor pains on a pregnant woman, and they will not escape. 4 But you, brothers, are not in darkness so that this day should surprise you like a thief.* 5 You are all sons of the light and sons of the day. We do not belong to the night or to the darkness. 6 *So then, let us not be like others, who are asleep, but let us be alert and self-controlled.* 7 For those who sleep, sleep at night, and those who get drunk, get drunk at night. 8 *But since we belong to the*

> *day, let us be self-controlled, putting on faith and love as a breastplate, and the hope of salvation as a helmet.* 9 For God did not appoint us to suffer wrath but to receive salvation through our Lord Jesus Christ. 10 He died for us so that, whether we are awake or asleep, we may live together with Him. 11 *Therefore encourage one another and build each other up, just as in fact you are doing.* (1Thess. 5:1–11, niv; emphasis added)

There are some very interesting thoughts in this section of scripture, especially when you apply them to our current society. This section of scripture is usually attributed to the tribulation period of time because it is speaking of the day of the Lord. It could also include the time that builds up to this consummation. Jesus said we would be able to recognize this time as it is approaching. He referred to it as "the beginning of birth pains" (Matthew 24:8). In verses 4–7, he gave a list of numerous things that would be happening in the season preceding what we understand to be the tribulation. Since Jesus said there would be a building of problems, distresses, wars, etc., could it be that what Paul is pointing out to the Thessalonian church is also part of that season? Let's look at the scriptures and see if they could apply today.

Verse 3. Peace and safety. This is describing a perspective or attitude. It's one of lethargy. We're safe. Nothing is going to happen to us. I'm not sure about other parts of the industrialized world, but this is a good description of the present attitude in America. Even after the attacks on the World Trade Center on September 11, 2001—and the many ongoing threats against our land—the consensus of the general public would almost seem to be, "Ignore it; it'll go away. It's not our problem." It's a very self-centered attitude and posturing.

Is it possible the destruction that Paul is talking about here has to do with the spirit of Antichrist and the selfishness that is gripping this world? The moral fabric, basic standards of morality, and any significant emphasis on Jesus and the Bible being a viable standard for society are quickly being eroded in America. This will lead to only one thing—destruction.

Verse 4–5. True believers who are led by the Holy Spirit should be well aware of what's happening and see it coming.

Verse 6. With that in mind, wake up to what's going on, be alert, and exercise some self-control.

Verse 8. In this verse, Paul is using armor as an illustration. Be self-controlled and put on your armor. Why would he be telling us to do this? Because the believer and the church need to take a stand concerning the things Paul mentions: faith, love, and salvation. Paul is inferring this could be a fight, so put on your armor.

Verse 11. Get into an agreement, encourage each other, and build each other up during this time. The Holy Spirit would not have spoken through Paul and said this if we didn't need it. To *encourage* is to put courage into another person, build them up, and help them to be strong. Why would he say that if there is not heavy opposition? We are seeing this opposition building around us on a daily basis.

"May God himself, the God of peace, sanctify you through and through. *May your whole spirit, soul and body be kept blameless at the coming of our Lord Jesus Christ.* The one who calls you is faithful, and He will do it" (1 Thess. 5:23–24, niv; emphasis added). Paul's prayer is that believers are blameless at Christ's return. With everything that Paul knew society and the church would be like before Jesus returns, this prayer indicates to me that Paul was concerned that believers would not be living this Christian life as they should. They will have gotten off somehow. It doesn't take a genius to see the church in America is off course. She is really going nowhere but is adrift in the seas of complacency, tolerance, inclusiveness, etc. (the Antichrist spirit). Is Christianity in America even pursuing the main reason Jesus said he came, "For the son of Man came to seek and to save what was lost" (Luke 19:10, niv)? Or are we so busy trying to be inclusive of all religions, beliefs, and faiths that we no longer see our society lost and in need of a savior. Understanding what motivated Paul, via his writings, I don't think he'd call that attitude blameless.

> 1 Concerning the coming of our Lord Jesus Christ and our being gathered to Him, we ask you, brothers, 2 not to become easily unsettled or alarmed by some

prophecy, report or letter supposed to have come from us, saying that the day of the Lord has already come. 3 Don't let anyone deceive you in any way, for *[that day will not come] until the rebellion occurs and the man of lawlessness is revealed*, the man doomed to destruction. 4 *He will oppose and will exalt himself over everything that is called God or is worshiped*, so that he sets himself up in God's temple, proclaiming himself to be God. 5 Don't you remember that when I was with you I used to tell you these things? 6 *And now you know what is holding him back, so that he may be revealed at the proper time. 7 For the secret power of lawlessness is already at work; but the one who now holds it back will continue to do so till he is taken out of the way.* 8 And then the lawless one will be revealed, whom the Lord Jesus will overthrow with the breath of his mouth and destroy by the splendor of His coming. 9 *The coming of the lawless one will be in accordance with the work of Satan displayed in all kinds of counterfeit miracles, signs and wonders, 10 and in every sort of evil that deceives those who are perishing. They perish because they refused to love the truth and so be saved.* 11 For this reason God sends them a powerful delusion so that they will believe the lie 12 and so that all will be condemned who have not believed the truth but have delighted in wickedness. 13 But we ought always to thank God for you, brothers loved by the Lord, because from the beginning God chose you to be saved through

the sanctifying work of the Spirit and through belief in
the truth. (2 Thess. 2:1–13,niv; emphasis added)

This particular passage has a lot of information in it.
It's definitely talking about the End Times, the Antichrist
spirit, and the man called Antichrist. Paul describes some of
the characteristics that will be in society at this time. Let's
look at a few of them:

Verse 3. The coming of Jesus won't happen until a few
things occur:

- The rebellion takes place.
- The man of lawlessness is revealed.

We have already shown that the man of lawlessness is
the Antichrist. We've already talked about the rebellion in
chapter 5. But I think it is worth repeating here. The niv
translates (G646: *apóstasia*) as rebellion. This is a poor
translation. It should be *falling away* or *apostasy*.

> *Strong's Dictionary*: 646. ἀποστασία apóstasia, ap-os-tas-ee'-ah; Feminine of the same as 647; *defection from truth* (properly the state), ("apostasy"). :— *falling away, forsake.* (emphasis added)

The *Amplified version* bares that out: "Let no one deceive
or beguile you in any way, for that day will not come except
the apostasy comes first [unless *the predicted great falling away*

of those who have professed to be Christians has come], and the man of lawlessness (sin) is revealed, who is the son of doom (of perdition), [Da 7:25; 8:25; 1 Ti 4:1]" (2 Thess. 2:3, amp; emphasis added).

There is a forsaking of the truth or falling away from Christianity that will take place during the time before the Antichrist is revealed. We are seeing that happen in society right now. Here is an excerpt from an article that shows what the next new thing in the American religious culture will be.

> End Of The American Dream
>
> New Trend: 'Radically Inclusive' Churches That Embrace All Religions And All Lifestyles
> By Michael Snyder, on March 24th, 2015
>
> If you want as many people to attend your church as possible, why limit yourself to just Christians? All over America, "radically inclusive" churches that embrace all religions and all lifestyles are starting to pop up. Church services that incorporate elements of Hinduism, Islam, Native American religions and even Wicca are becoming increasingly common. And even if you don't believe anything at all, that is okay with these churches too. In fact, as you will see below, one Presbyterian minister in Oregon is even inviting people to "bring their own god" to church. But if these churches don't really stand for anything at all, what is their purpose? And what does the

popularity of these churches say about the future of religion in America?

The questions at the end of that excerpt are very pertinent. What is the church in America doing? I can see this becoming a popular trend. In reality, it's another step lower in the ongoing push by the spirit of Antichrist toward the demise of Christianity in this world. It's an obvious departure or falling away from the truth of the gospel. It would be nice if it were going to be a small passing thing, but if the *Amplified* translation is correct, it will be a "great falling away."

This is happening in our time.It's picking up momentum. I share Paul's concern for the salvation of the human race.

Verse 4. If this is what the man Antichrist is going to do, why will it be accepted by the public? We already answered that question, but I'll say it again. It will be acceptable because the spirit of Antichrist will have paved the way for it. Society will already be preconditioned to accept it. We are watching it happen around us on a daily basis. Things that are of God are openly being opposed, and the things that are not of God are being exalted. People are used to it and too often agree with it. The Antichrist will easily be able to take advantage of this degenerate society and literally ride the wave of lawlessness into power.

Verses 6–7. There is only one thing that holds the power of lawlessness in check. It is the power of righteousness. And righteousness is exalted through Godly people. The less people take a stand on true godliness, the less

The Breath of Anti-Christ

withholding or restraining power there is. It is the person who is a true sold-out believer in Jesus the Christ and who is willing to make a stand for what is righteous that this verse is talking about.

Verse 9. Supernatural things that are rooted in an evil and ungodly source will be very prominent in the last days. There will be many counterfeit miracles, signs, and wonders that will be done through people who are absolutely anti the Christ. Just because it's supernatural doesn't automatically mean it is of our God or from his heavenly kingdom. This will demand the leading and anointing of the Holy Spirit so we can discern the true from the false. Just like in 1 John 2, believers will desperately need the anointing to recognize what is really going on around them. The Holy Spirit and the purpose for which He was sent is absolutely essential in the last days. That's why God said, "In the last days...I will pour my Spirit out on all people" (Acts 2:17, niv). He has been given for our time.

Verse 10. Evil will continue to rise. It will be viewed as normal by the majority (just like it is now). The worst part of it is the deception of people. It will continue to delude and deceive the people who are perishing—the people not filled with and following the Holy Spirit. It's not that truth isn't available. It *is* available, but the spirit of Antichrist, selfishness, and lawlessness has taken such a prominent position of influence in the earth that many, many people will refuse to accept the truth.

Verses 11–12. So, as in Romans 1, God will give them what they so desire. He will give them a powerful delusion so they can have what they want—to believe the lie. The result is the loss of their salvation.

Verse 13. For believers, there is good news. The Holy Spirit is still at work in anyone who wants to see the truth and serve the living God. He will work in them to sanctify them. *Sanctify* means to be "separated from the world and set apart to God." *Notice, the Holy Spirit is at work.* He is at work in the people who will welcome Him. And it will be through the work of the Holy Spirit and the Word of God/Truth (John 17:17, Galatians 1:5, 1 Timothy 2:15), people who choose to believe will be saved.

Don't lose heart. It's not all lost. God is still on the throne and he is faithful. Everyone who calls on the name of the Lord will still be saved (Romans 10:13). The Holy Spirit will still be doing his work on the earth. However, I do believe to find the truth and to spiritually stay on course will take more focus because deception will lay across this earth like a thick fog. But rest assured, those who seek Jesus with their whole heart will find him.

It's interesting how that once we see truth, the scriptures take on a different light. For example what Paul said in 1 Thessalonians chapter 5, verse 6 as he was giving his warnings concerning the time surrounding the coming of the Lord. He said: So then, let us not be like others, who are asleep, but let us be alert and self-controlled (niv). The kjv says: Watch and be sober. With deception being so thick in this time, it makes sense that the Holy Spirit would say that we need to be alert, watch, and be self-controlled and stay sober.

9

My Concern

The time into which we are entering is not something to be taken lightly.

The main thing that we need to be seeing can be summed up in one word—selfishness. That word is the key that unlocks the question of, "How did we get to this point?" We got here because we turned selfish and lawless. These two are cloaked in many deceptive terms. Selfishness and lawlessness are actively working among us while being disguised as tolerance, acceptance, love, enlightenment, grace, freedom in Christ, the new move of the twenty-first century, a user-friendly gospel, etc. In reality, I believe we are being led down a path that will ultimately end in destruction for many people. And in too many cases, the one who is leading us is not the Holy Spirit. It is the spirit of Antichrist. The horrible reality is that we as a people have gotten so out of step with the Holy Spirit and insensitive to His voice and leading that the Holy Spirit is not able to show the average Christian in America the reality of what's happening around them.

Because of the increase of wickedness and the pressure of the ungodly spirit realm around us, believers will be deceived into pursuing the wrong pursuits. However, they won't be recognized as the wrong pursuits (Matt. 24:37–39, 2 Tim. 3:1–4, Rev. 2–3). Christians and the Christian church will rationalize and excuse them away as being normal: "It's just the way it is" (2 Tim. 3:5).

As wickedness increases around us, and the love for God and the things of God grows cold, many will find themselves being pulled further into a deception and lose faith (Matthew 24:4, 10–12; Luke 18:8).

We will watch believers become very selfish (2 Tim. 3:1–5). What God considers to be merely pleasures and amusements will become the main focus of our lives, and we will plan our lives around these things more than we are planning around God and what He desires (2 Tim. 3:4).

In our opinions, we're still Christians, but the proof that we have fallen into this deception will be the attitude and reality of spiritual powerlessness (2 Tim. 3:5), or the *power* not being active in our lives.

That word for power is *dunamis*. That's the power of Acts 1:8. If that power is not active in believer's lives, that means the Holy Spirit is also not active in their lives because that power flows from the Spirit.

The Breath of Anti-Christ

Not only will the power not be active, but believers will actually take a definite stand against it. The manifestations of the Spirit and His power will receive less and less credence. In its place will grow a very powerless religious people who will scorn and mock those who stand for the true power of the Holy Spirit. Since the Holy Spirit *always* points to Jesus, this will again be an attack on Jesus, another form of denying him.

The main point of attack will be against Jesus. It's because of Him that people are persecuted (Matthew 24:9). It will be those who take a stand for Him and persist in the belief that *Jesus is the only Savior and Messiah for the people of this world* who will be singled out and labeled. They will be regarded as evil, anti-society, intolerant, a menace regarding the good of this world, narrow-minded, and a threat to the peace because of their opinionated extremist views. The day will come that society will consider a person Godly or to be a true Christian if they are silent about sin and simply go along with and tolerate any and every belief and doctrine. Every effort will be made to do away with the true conviction/convincing of the Holy Spirit. In order to do that, the people who are still the salt and light of the world will need to be squelched.

I don't believe we are ready for this type of persecution. My concern is that we are being lulled to sleep by the complacency, lethargy, and the push for tolerance and universalism that is taking place in the world. Specifically in

America, our children have been raised with such comfort and ease that I am concerned whether they will have the spiritual wherewithal to take the stand required to retain their salvation. To be quite honest, I am not convinced the adults who call themselves Christians in America have what it takes to withstand this type of persecution.

I know that God is always faithful and that the Holy Spirit will be actively working on every human being in this earth. I pray that everything we have been hearing about a great last- days revival and harvest is accurate. However, my concern is what Jesus and Paul had to say about the huge number of people who will grow cold and fall away from Christianity.

> Because of the increase of wickedness, *the love of most will grow cold.* (Mt 24:12, niv; emphasis added)
>
> Let no one deceive or beguile you in any way, for that day will not come except the apostasy comes first [unless *the predicted great falling away of those who have professed to be Christians* has come], and the man of lawlessness (sin) is revealed, who is the son of doom (of perdition). (2 Thess. 2:3, amp)

Is the church going to follow the same pattern the Israelites did in the Old Testament? What I mean by that is this: will there be only a remnant who are saved while the majority of people who knew about God, his Word, the Holy Spirit, Jesus being the Savior, etc. grow cold and fall away from God because they have bought into the deception of the Antichrist spirit? Is it possible that the great harvest and revival that is to take place on this earth may gather in millions of new believers while those who already had the gospel are turning their back on it?

I say it again: the time of the last days into which we are entering is not something to be taken lightly. There is a reason for the many, many scriptural warnings concerning this period of time. I think we would do well to pay attention to and heed the warnings.

10

What's the Answer?

What's the answer to all of this? What do we do so we can come out from under the influence of the Antichrist system? How can we ensure we are not deceived? What do we do to ensure our lineage (children, grandchildren, great-grandchildren, etc.) don't fall into deception?

There's an old saying that goes like this: "Recognizing there is a problem is half of the solution." This land and many parts of the world need a spiritual awakening. And the only one who can awaken the church and the world is God. If God (the Father, Jesus, and the Holy Spirit) can't get through to us, no one else will.

We could give many answers to the questions listed above, but I believe the greatest answer is the one we've already been talking about. It's the Holy Spirit. He is the only one who can give us true wisdom. He is the only one who can help us clearly see the deception that is surrounding us. He is the only one capable of guiding and leading us through this time. That's why Acts 2 and the outpouring of the Holy Spirit is connected to the last days (Acts 2:17).

The book of Jude gives us specific instructions as to what we should do to stay on track in the last days.

> 17 But, dear friends, remember what the apostles of our Lord Jesus Christ foretold. 18 They said to you, "*In the last times* there will be scoffers who will *follow their own ungodly desires.*" 19 These are the men who divide you, *who follow mere natural instincts and do not have the Spirit.* 20 *But you, dear friends, build yourselves up in your most holy faith and pray in the Holy Spirit.* 21 *Keep yourselves in God's love as you wait* for the mercy of our Lord Jesus Christ to bring you to eternal life. 22 *Be merciful to those who doubt; 23 snatch others from the fire and save them; to others show mercy, mixed with fear—hating even the clothing stained by corrupted flesh. 24 To him who is able to keep you from falling and to present you before his glorious presence without fault and with great joy—25 to the only God our Savior* be glory, majesty, power and authority, through *Jesus Christ our Lord*, before all ages, now and forevermore! Amen. (Jude 1:17–25, niv; emphasis added)

Here Jude is the one who expresses concerns concerning the last days. Here again the characteristic of selfishness and a couple of the ways it will influence society are being pointed out (vv. 18–19). Jude also gives some very specific input concerning this time. He tells the following:

The Breath of Anti-Christ

1. Build ourselves and keep ourselves strong in the faith (v. 20).
2. Pray in the Holy Spirit (v. 20).
3. Keep ourselves in God's love (v. 21).
4. Be merciful to those who doubt (v. 22).
5. Snatch others from the fire and save them (v. 23).
6. Show mercy mixed with *fear* (Gr. *alarm*) (v. 23).
7. Return to a true recognition of the corruption of the flesh and sin. Hating not only what it does to the person, but hating even the stain it leaves on their lives (clothing) (v. 23).
8. Return to putting our full trust and faith in *the only one* (there is no other Savior) who can present us before the Father without fault and with joy—Jesus Christ our Lord (vv. 24–25).

We need to be alarmed at what is going on around us (Jude 23). The society we are living in *should not seem normal*. It has the stench of Antichrist all over it. We need to ask the Holy Spirit to help us see it for what it is. We must recognize what's going on, or we will slide even further into deception.

The time in which we are living should not be taken lightly. We need to be aware of what we're facing. That's why Jesus, Paul, Peter, John, and Jude all warned about this time. It needs to be taken very seriously. But we also don't want to become fearful about it. Jude points out in verse 24–25 that this is not too big for God. He is capable of dealing with this time and getting His people through it "without fault and with great joy." In the book of 1 John, where we find some of the most detailed information concerning the Antichrist in the entire New Testament, we find John specifically addressing the issue of fear. In chapter 4, right after showing us how to test for the spirit of Antichrist, he deals with love and fear.

> 7 Dear friends, let us love one another, for love comes from God. Everyone who loves has been born of God and knows God. 8 Whoever does not love does not know God, because God is love. 9 This is how God showed his love among us: He sent his one and only Son into the world that we might live through him. 10 This is love: not that we loved God, but that he loved us and sent his Son as an atoning sacrifice for our sins. 11 Dear friends, since God so loved us, we also ought to love one another. 12 No one has ever seen God; but if we love one another, God lives in us and his love is made complete in us. 13 *We know that we live in him and he in us, because he has given us of his Spirit.* 14 And we have seen and testify that the Father has sent his Son to be the Savior of the world. 15 If anyone acknowledges that Jesus is the Son of God, God lives in him and he in God. 16 And so we know and rely on the love God

> has for us. *God is love. Whoever lives in love lives in God, and God in him.* 17 *In this way, love is made complete among us so that we will have confidence on the day of judgment,* because in this world we are like him. 18 *There is no fear in love. But perfect love drives out fear, because fear has to do with punishment. The one who fears is not made perfect in love.* 19 We love because He first loved us. (1 Jn 4:7–19, niv; emphasis added)

Because of God's love for us, we have nothing to fear. In fact, His love will drive all fear out of us. The directive John is giving to us is that we need to grow in that love. So I need to point it out again: this is the exact opposite of what "lawlessness" will try to produce in us (Matthew 24:12). Selfishness and lawlessness cause our love for God to grow cold. John says the exact opposite is needed to get through this time. We need to grow in and be more secure in God's love than ever. It will drive any fear right out of us. So no matter what the Antichrist spirit may be causing, or whatever may be happening in the world in the last days, as we press into the love of God (moving away from lawlessness and selfishness), fear will have a diminishing hold on the believer, ultimately, growing to the point of no fear whatsoever.

Just in case you hadn't noticed, the Holy Spirit is again mentioned in Jude 20 and 1 John 4:13, where they are talking about the last days and what we should do during this time. Having a personal relationship with the Holy Spirit and letting Him do His work in us is going to be vital for anyone to be victorious in the last days. He's been given to help us in the last days. It is absolutely essential that we avail ourselves of who's been given to us—the Holy Spirit.

Learn how to talk to Him, listen to Him, and become intimate with Him. Pursue relationship with Him. Seek after it on a daily basis. Realize that He is an invisible companion who is with us 24 hours a day, 7 days a week, 365 days a year. The entire purpose for which He was sent to this earth was to bring people to the Savior—Jesus—and then live with and in these believers to help them through this life and into an eternity in heaven. Once we are born- again, the Holy Spirit has no other purpose in us than to do whatever is necessary to help the believer.

Learn to recognize His presence. Know what it feels like. It cannot be imitated and faked. In His presence, you will find peace, wisdom, counsel, power, understanding, knowledge, and the true awe of who God really is (Isaiah 11:2). In Him, you will find counsel, comfort, truth, and companionship (John 14:15–21). He will convince you of what is sinful and wrong, righteous and correct, and that there is nothing that can stop you from doing what He wants. The devil has been tried and condemned. He has no power over you as a believer (John 16:5–11). He will work with you at the pace you can handle. He will speak to you, lead you, guide you into all truth, tell you what Jesus desires, reveal to you what is coming in the future, and give you insight into the Father and Jesus—how they think, their perspective, what they think you should do, and anything else that is theirs that they would like you to have or know about. He will give you the ability to accurately see what Jesus is like (John 16:12–16).

There is no companion who is more trustworthy, faithful, reliable, intelligent, knowledgeable, wise, comforting, encouraging, loving, patient, kind, joyful, peaceful, insightful, good, gentle, and self-disciplined than the Holy Spirit. Get to know Him on a conversational level. Pursue intimacy with Him like He is God and has decided to be with you and help you for your whole life because He *is* and *has*.

As you do, you'll learn to recognize His voice, sense His presence, understand and work with His anointing, and follow His leading. He will keep you safe like no other can. You won't be deceived.

11

What is Our Hope?

It's in the settings of persecution and trouble that the Gospel, Christianity, the working and moving of the Holy Spirit flourishes. In history, persecution and difficult times have always propelled the true church of Jesus Christ to heights that would have been otherwise unattainable. I had a teacher in Bible college who compared it to a fire. He said when the fire of the Holy Spirit begins to burn in people, to stop it is almost impossible. No matter how much you try to put it out, it's like stomping on a fire. The more you stomp on it, the further it spreads. The sparks fly everywhere and ignite everything that they touch. When God is set free to "burn" in a person, church, or nation, there is no putting Him out.

It's sad that we have to get to that place of trouble and persecution before we'll allow God to do what He wants. If truth be known, we wouldn't have to get into that situation. God is more than willing to do great things among us right now. But if there's one thing God was concerned about with His people Israel—and we saw his concern validated—it was that when things were good, they forgot about Him. When life becomes easy, human beings tend to forget about their need for God. If it takes some hard times to get mankind's attention again, so be it. Even in recent history—take 9/11 as an example—when life becomes difficult, people are more inclined to reach out to God.

The church in America, and some other parts of the world, needs to come out from under its slumber and the

> The Word must be given preeminence once again in the church, and we must return to viewing our lives through the filter of the scripture rather than viewing the scripture through the filter of society.

deception that has gotten on too much of it. There needs to be an awakening of the people of God. The preachers need to return to preaching righteousness, holiness, and that there is a standard against which the church and the believer needs to be measured. It is not the standard of this world. It is the standard of the scripture. If the future generations are going to be saved, the Word of God needs to be returned to its rightful place in the life of believers and the church.

The Word of God is the standard we measure ourselves against. It is God-breathed and useful for teaching, rebuking, correcting, and training in righteousness (2 Timothy 3:16). In it is everything we need for life and godliness. It contains the great and precious promises that are able to help us escape the corruption in the world caused by evil desires (selfishness—2 Peter 1:3–4). The Word must be given preeminence once again in the church, and we must return to viewing our lives through the filter of the scripture rather than viewing the scripture through the filter of society. Scriptural guidelines and standards must never conform to the wisdom of our society and this world. Rather, this world and society need to conform to what God has laid out for guidelines and standards, and I'm not talking about any and every so-called god in this world. I'm talking about the God of the Bible.

For the Bible to once again have a premium placed on it, we will need to return to the Holy Spirit who is described in the New Testament as the one of wisdom, power, and authority; the Spirit of the supernatural—dreams, visions, signs, wonders, and gifts; the Spirit who has a 24–7 active relationship with the people of God. We need to once again learn how to hear His voice clearly and consistently. To be led, instructed, trained, helped, reminded, counseled, convicted, convinced, encouraged, and guided by Him.

He is the only One capable of bringing the scripture to life and making it live in our lives. Without His help, the human being is incapable of understanding what the Word really has to say. Without His help, we cannot understand the scripture or any Godly spiritual thing (1 Corinthians 2:6–16). That is probably the greatest single reason the church is in the poor spiritual condition it is currently in. In too many denominations and churches, the Holy Spirit has been removed from His rightful position of authority, power, and instruction. He has been demoted to someone we speak about in a creed but is no longer a living, breathing, active, integral, and essential person in our life that we have learned to hear, speak to, receive direction from, be encouraged by, and follow as we go through this earthly life.

Believers need to become intimately acquainted with Him once again.

There is a reason Jesus said it was absolutely necessary for Him to return to heaven: so that the Holy Spirit would be given. Our hope as individuals, churches, nations, and the world lies in the Word and that Holy Spirit (Romans 15:4, 13).

> We need to once again learn how to hear His voice clearly and consistently.
> To be led, instructed, trained, helped, reminded, counseled, convicted, convinced, encouraged, and guided by Him.

For those believers who will embrace those two sources of hope with everything that is within them, there will be nothing that can make them hopeless. The Bible is full of promises to God's people who pursue Him with all their heart, soul, mind, and strength. So let's pursue!

I will end this book with a few of those promises:

> But as surely as God is faithful, our message to you is not "Yes" and "No." For the Son of God, Jesus Christ, who was preached among you by me and Silas and Timothy, was not "Yes" and "No," but in Him it has always been "Yes." For no matter how many promises God has made, they are "Yes" in Christ. And so through Him the "Amen" is spoken by us to the glory of God. Now it is God who makes both us and you stand firm in Christ. He anointed us, set his seal of ownership on us, and put his Spirit in our hearts as a deposit, guaranteeing what is to come. (2 Cor 1:18–22, niv)

> But thanks be to God, who always leads us in triumphal procession in Christ and through us spreads everywhere the fragrance of the knowledge of him. (2 Cor 2:14, niv)

> So do not throw away your confidence; it will be richly rewarded. You need to persevere so that when you have done the will of God, you will receive what He has promised. For in just a very little while, "He who is coming will come and will not delay. But my righteous one will live by faith. And if he shrinks back, I will not be pleased with him." But we are not of

those who shrink back and are destroyed, but of those who believe and are saved. (Heb 10:35–39, (niv)

But before all this, they will lay hands on you and persecute you. They will deliver you to synagogues and prisons, and you will be brought before kings and governors, and all on account of My name. This will result in your being witnesses to them. But make up your mind not to worry beforehand how you will defend yourselves. For I will give you words and wisdom that none of your adversaries will be able to resist or contradict. You will be betrayed even by parents, brothers, relatives and friends, and they will put some of you to death. All men will hate you because of me. But not a hair of your head will perish. By standing firm you will save yourselves. (Lk 21:12–19, niv)

When these things begin to take place, stand up and lift up your heads, because your redemption is drawing near. (Lk 21:28, niv)

[B]eing confident of this, that He who began a good work in you will carry it on to completion until the day of Christ Jesus. (Phil 1:6, niv)

Now there is in store for me the crown of righteousness, which the Lord, the righteous Judge, will award to me on that day—and not only to me, but also to all who have longed for His appearing. (2 Tim. 4:8, niv)

> Now unto the King eternal, immortal, invisible, the
> only wise God, be honor and glory for ever and ever.
> Amen. (1 Tim. 1:17, kjv)

Verbally, ask Jesus to forgive your sins and commit your life to Him as your savior. Say this prayer: Jesus, I admit I am a sinner. I ask you to forgive me. Be my Lord and my Master. I submit myself to you as being the only true savior of this world. I believe you came to this earth, died for my sins, and rose from the dead. I choose to serve and follow you with all my heart, and with my mouth I declare you to be my Lord. I ask for the Baptism in the Holy Spirit. You said I need him to help me, so I receive the fullness of the Holy Spirit to work with me in whatever way he sees is best. Thank-You. I put my trust in you as my savior.

If you have, continue; if you haven't, begin to study the Bible and allow the Holy Spirit to point out many more of the promises that have been made to you.

Be blessed, and until we meet over there, pursue your God with all your heart, soul, mind, and strength. No matter what it may cost you—remain faithful to Him.

Contact Information:

Vern Peltz
wordoflifemn.org

Made in the USA
Monee, IL
25 August 2020